LANDSCAPES OF ISRAEL

DRAWINGS BY

MOSHE KAUFMAN

Plates by : H. S. Halfi Ltd. OR-YEHUDA

Printed by : TOP PRINT Ltd. TEL-AVIV

ISBN 965 - 90603 - 0 - 0

PRINTED IN ISRAEL 2003

Published by : M. KAUFMAN - 15 sharet st., Tel-aviv 62092, Israel

Fax : 972 - 3 - 6963039 e–mail : mosheko@zahav.net.il

CONTENTS

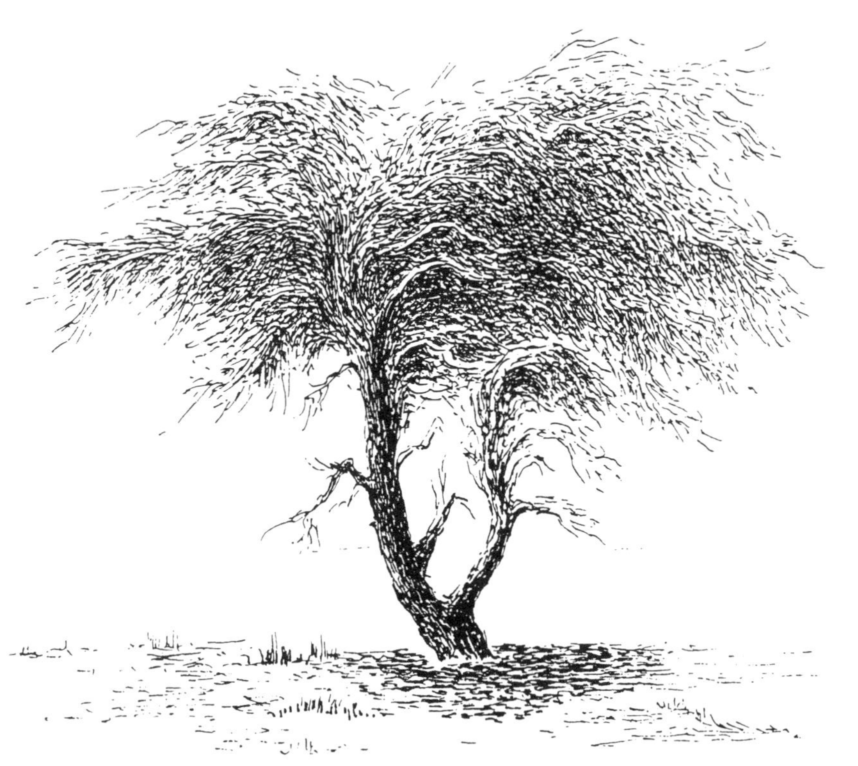

INTRODUCTION

This collection of drawings in “Black and White”- selected from hundreds of drawings - is the fruition of sketching trips to the historic and picturesque landscapes of the Holy Land. They reflect my inspiration from visiting Jerusalem, Judea, the Galilee, the Negev and the Arava.

In 1949, one year after the founding of the State of Israel and after the outbreak of Israel’s independence war, the Israel Defence Force conquered the south of the Negev and the region of Eilat. Shortly after that I was appointed the Town Planner of the future city of Eilat.
In those days the area was desolate and desert-like and the only structure in the area was a courtyard with a small number of dirty rooms that used to serve as a police station known by the name of “Um-Rashrash”.
This desolate courtyard was located on the shore of a beautiful dark-blue bay which was surrounded by lovely colored mountains.

The task of planning the City of Eilat tied me for four years to the historic and exciting chapter of planning the country from the beginning.
Since this job required numerous tours in and around this part of country, I had the wanderful chance to discover that world of fascinating desert landscapes, rocky mountains and sandy valleys. These views enchanted me more and more and spurred me on to absorb and draw these mysterious and virgin landscapes.

Of all the various techniques, I most prefer to paint in black and white. It gives me the most satisfaction and an opportunity for greater expression. I used to compare colored painting to the performance of an orchestra playing with all its instruments, while drawing in black and white is compared to the gentle music of the unaccompanied soloist, where each note and each dot has its own unique value and importance.

Moshe Kaufman

Moshe Kaufman ..... with only pen and ink on paper, he paints the simple country scenes that are wholly a part of him, and the intensity with which they are felt, make them rise off the page as from the page of the Old Testament. The simple jagged desert tree, with a few bushes and a hill behind them, is the stuff with which Moshe Kaufman can make magic.

Bruno Pulmer Poroner
"ARTSPEAK" New york

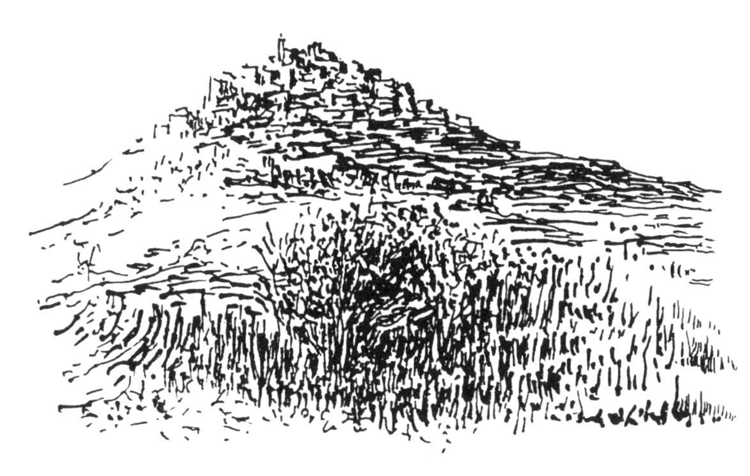

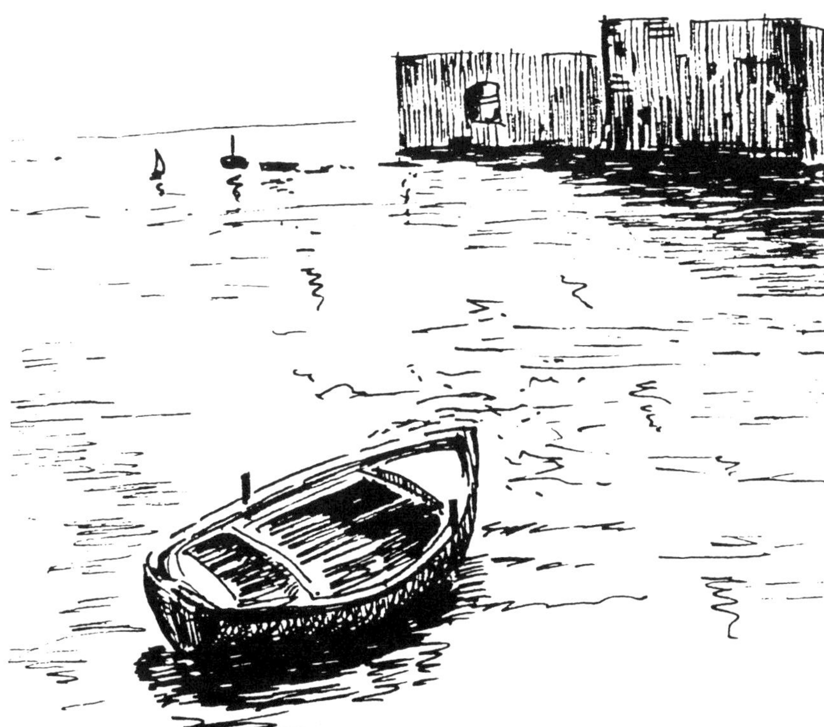

Moshe Kaufman's landscapes in black and white are drawn with a gentle and loving hand. In his drawings, mostly in rapid fluttery pen strokes, one can feel the artist's admiration of the magestic scenery.

Kaufman does not copy nature in a realistic style. He rather adopts an impressionist tinge with a personal touch. His work consist of mysticism and imagination combined with realism. His expressive landscapes reveal a concealed force of the artist as well as his inner truth that characterizes him.

Kaufman masters both composition and line. His paintings, while reminding us of the renderings of the impressionists, are always a part of his private soul.

"WORLD OF ART" Tel-aviv

Moshe Kaufman's visual integrity is the mature fruition of his search for a convincing idiom in which to describe those facets of nature – rocks, mountains, hills – of the Negev, Sinai, and Judea, which inspired his pen since childhood. His formative years were spent in Jerusalem, where his early and continuing preocupation with rocks and desert forms, as well as the urban landscapes of Jerusalem, was first nurtured. His student years in Haifa , with their sketching trips to the mountains of the Carmel range, and the Galilee in general, reaffirmed his absorption in those subjects which remain the core of his work today.

Later years, those in which Kaufman was involved in the planning and the building up of the town of Eilat, brought the artist into close and continuous contact with the mountainous desert landscapes of the Negev and the Arava.

Kaufman's drawings are a combination of painstaking and accurate observation, patiently annotated and well-composed. Their fluid surface maintains a complex play of line and mass in the moulding of dominant natural forms. His mercurial line darts and curves upon itself, sketching out the characteristic traits of the rocky landscapes. Sometimes stippled black strokes meet to mark out trees or bushes as well as boulders or terraced hillsides, as Kaufman searches for, and successfully defines the mountainous landscapes and desert formations which inspire his pen and brush alike.

….In his latest Negev views, Kaufman has extended and developed his pen and wash technique, giving an elegant and yet powerfully three dimensional rendering of the jagged summits of the desert with their peaks and gorges. The stark tonal contrasts of the desert environment remain a constant source of inspiration for Kaufman's fertile pen. His detailed and pleasing graphic accounts of the majestic peaks of the Negev and Sinai or the historic surroundings of Jerusalem, are a serious artist's response to the moving and difficult challenge of nature and history in the Land of Israel.

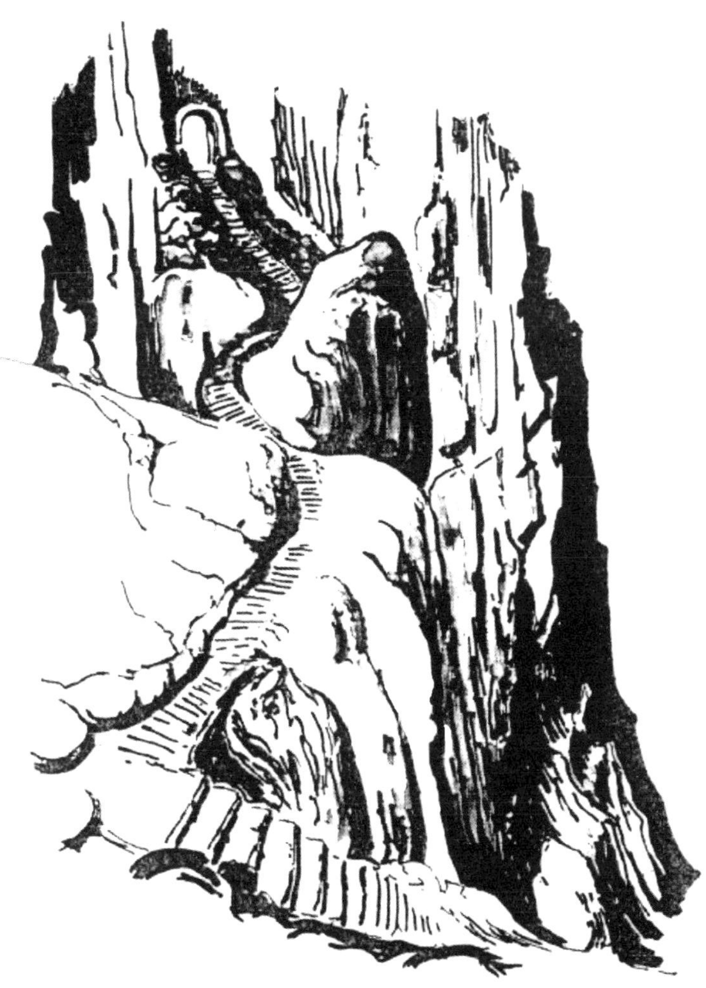

Sandra P. Heideecker
"WORD OF ART" Tel Aviv

J E R U S A L E M

LIST OF LANDSCAPES

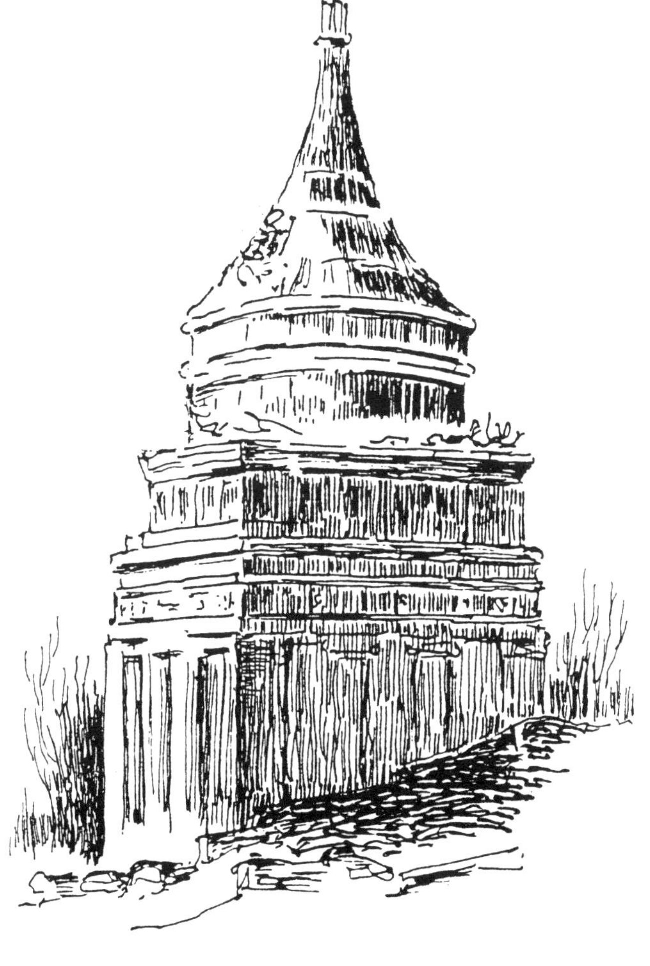

NAMES AND PLACES

Jerusalem was already mentioned in the ancient Egyptian Texts of the 19th – 18th centuries B.C. The city, also called Jebus, was conquered by King David who established the city as the capital of his kingdom **Judah.** Ever since then Jerusalem has always been the center of the Jewish people.

"DAVID WAS THIRTY YEARS OLD WHEN HE BEGAN TO REIGN, AND HE REINGNED FORTY YEARS. IN HEVRON HE REIGNED OVER JUDAH SEVEN YEARS AND SIX MONTHS , AND IN JERUSALEM HE REIGNED THIRTY THREE YEARS OVER ALL ISRAEL AND JUDAH." (2nd SAMUEL chapter 5 : 4-5)

The walls surrounding the Old City were built by the Turkish Sultan Suleiman the magnificent in the 16th century. They are roughly based on the walls built by the Romans who, in the 2nd century, rebuilt Jerusalem after the destruction of the city caused by their war against the Jews.

Mount of Olives : According to the Jewish belief that the Messiah will ascend the Mount of Olives and that the resurrection of the dead will take place, this part of the Mount of Olives have become a burial place for the Jews of Jerusalem. According to the New Testament the Ascension of Jesus occurred on the Mount of Olives.

"THE LORD WILL STAND IN THAT DAY ON THE MOUNT OF OLIVES, WHICH IS BEFORE JERUSALEMT ON THE EAST; AND THE MOUNT OF OLIVES WILL BE SPLIT IN TWO, FROM EAST TO WEST, MAKING A VERY GREAT VALLEY."
(ZECHARIAH chapter 14 : 4)

The Christian Quarter is one of the 4 quarters of the Old City. The other quarters are: Jewish, Moslem, and Armenian quarters.
Many famous churches are concentrated in the Christian Quarter:
The Holy Sepulchre, the Redeemer's Church, St. John the Buptist, St. Saviour Church, St. Michael Church and some others.

The Kidron Valley – between Mount of Olives and the Old City walls. Part of the valley is also known as the Valley of Jehoshaphat.

"...THE KING (DAVID) ALSO HIMSELF PASSED OVER THE BROOK KIDRON..''
(2ND SAMUEL chapter 15 : 23)

"...AND HE BROUGHT OUT THE GROVE FROM THE HOUSE OF THE LORD, WITHOUT JERUSALEM, UNTO THE BROOK OF KIDRON..."
(2ND KINGS Chapter 23:40)

Valley of Jehoshaphat – the upper part of the Kidron Valley between Mount of Olives and the walls of the Old City.
According to tradition it is believed that the Valley may be regarded as the Court-yard where God's final judgment on the enemies of Israel will take place.

"...I WILL ALSO GATHER ALL NATIONS, AND WILL BRING THEM DOWN INTO THE VALLEY OF JEHOSHAPHAT, AND WILL PLEAD WITH THEM THERE FOR MY PEOPLE AND FOR MY HERITAGE ISRAEL..."
(JOEL Chapter 3 : 2)

Absalom pillar : According to the Bible – Absalom (son of David) built a monument to himself during his lifetime.

"...NOW ABSALOM IN HIS LIFETIME HAD TAKEN AND REARED UP FOR HIMSELF THE PILLAR, WHICH IS IN THE KINGS DALE; FOR HE SAID, I HAVE NO SUN TO KEEP MY NAME IN MEMORY: AND HE CALLED THE PILLAR AFTER HIS OWN NAME; AND IT IS CALLED ABSALOM'S MONUMENT TO THIS DAY."
2ND SAMUEL Chapter 18 : 18)

Via Dolorosa - means "The Way of Sorrows". It refers to a pilgrim route in the Old City, that begins near the Lion's Gate and ends at the Holy Sepulchre. According to tradition this is the road Jesus took from the place of his condemnation to where he has been crucified.

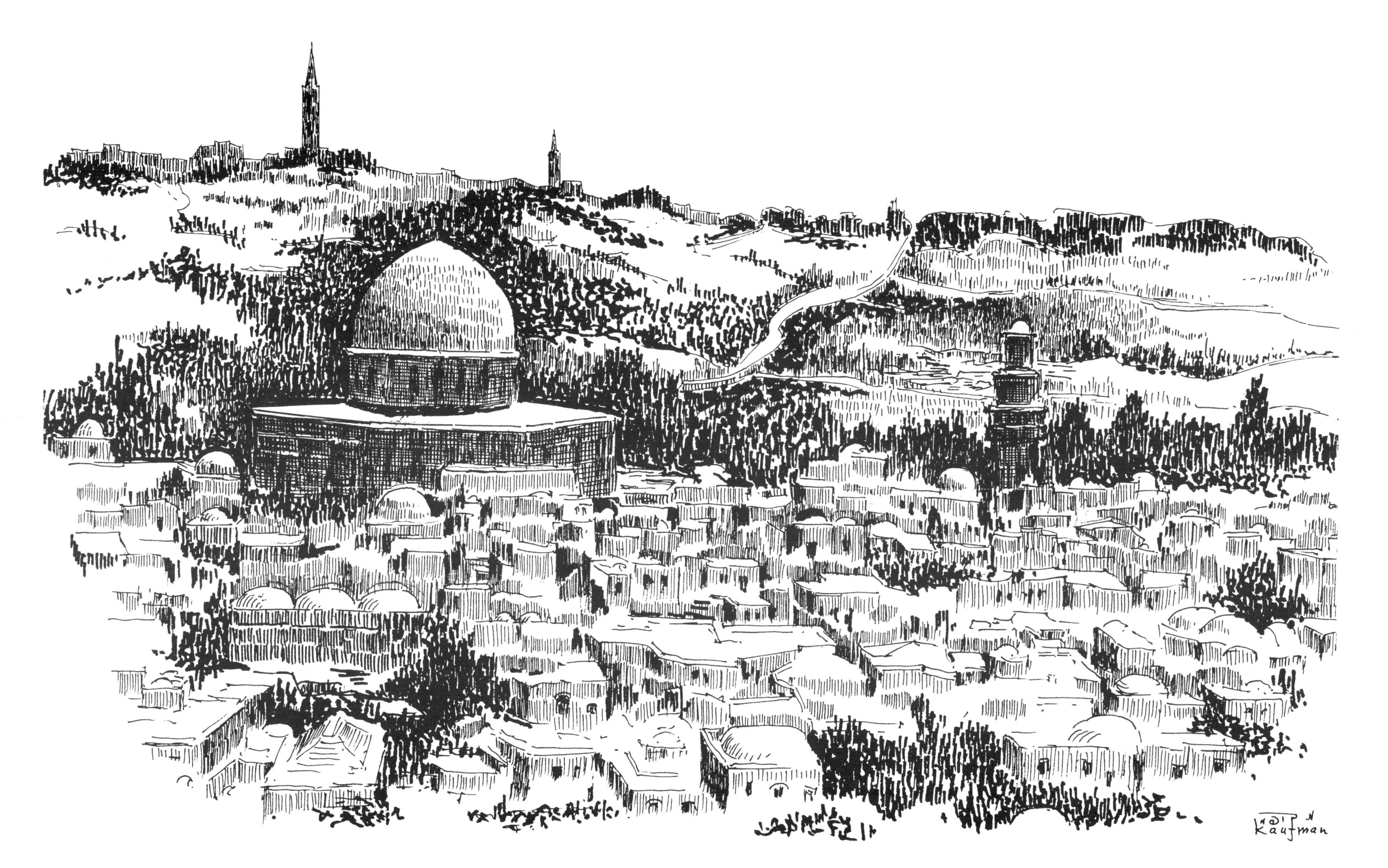
Kaufman

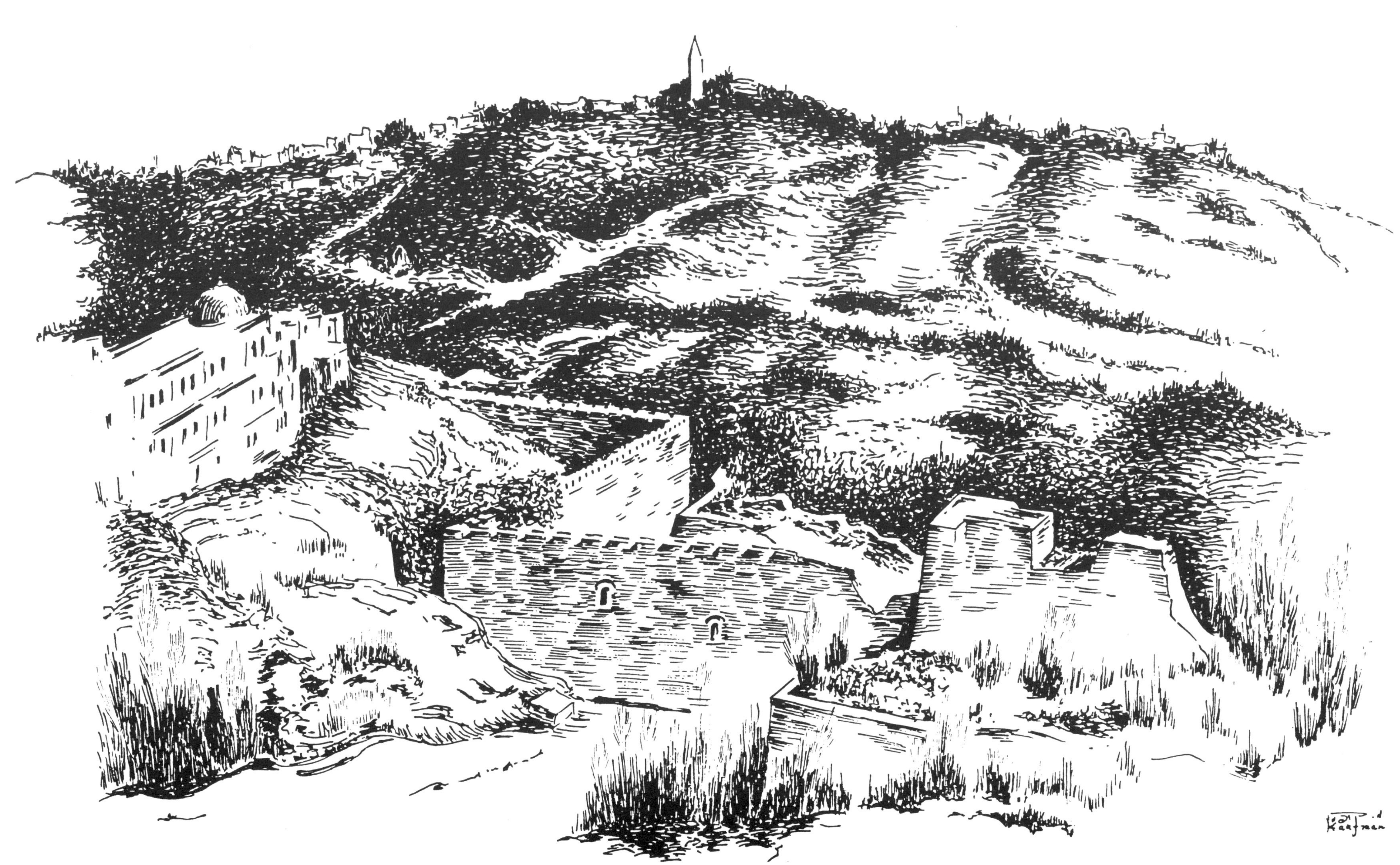

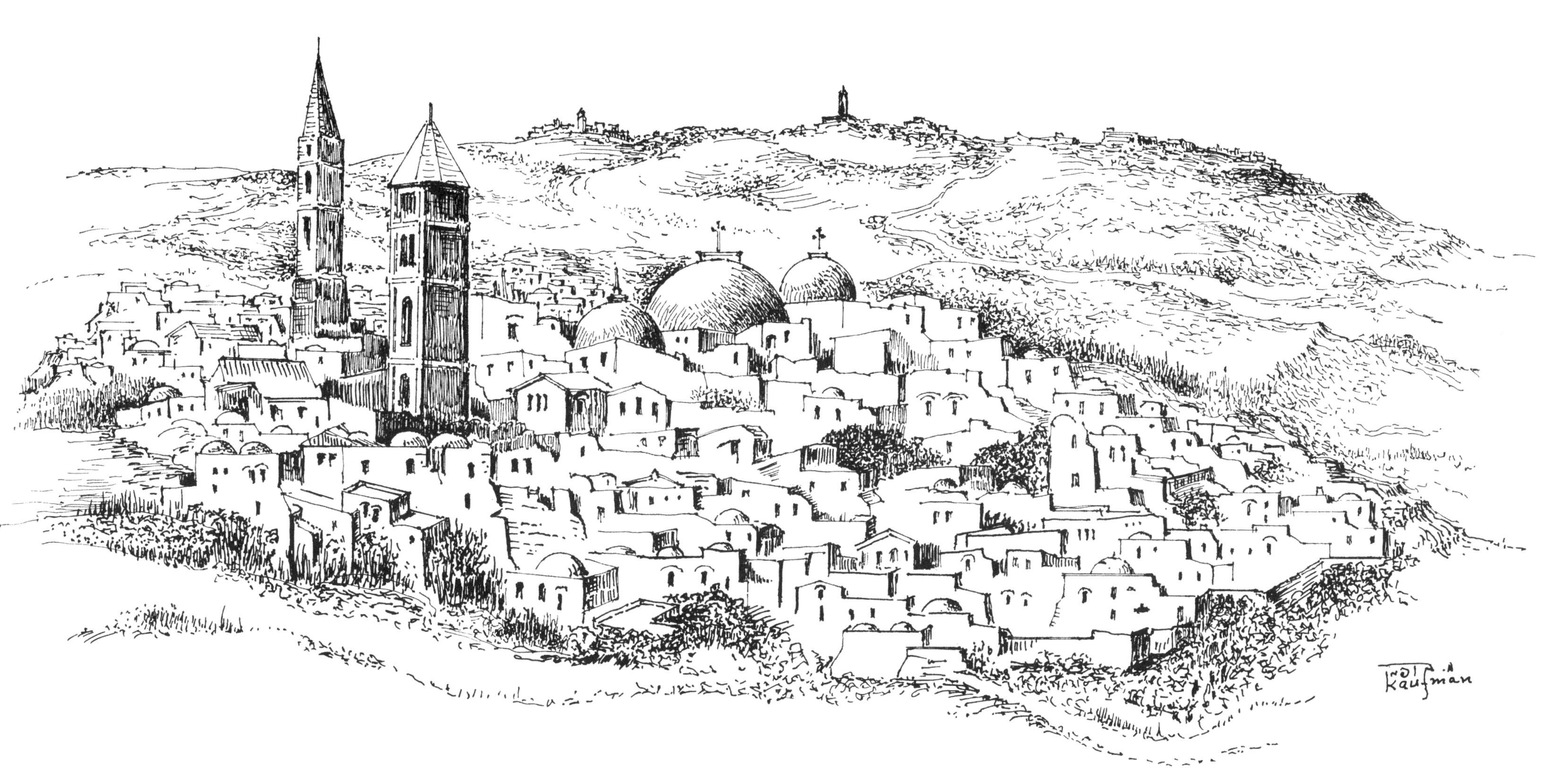
Kaufman

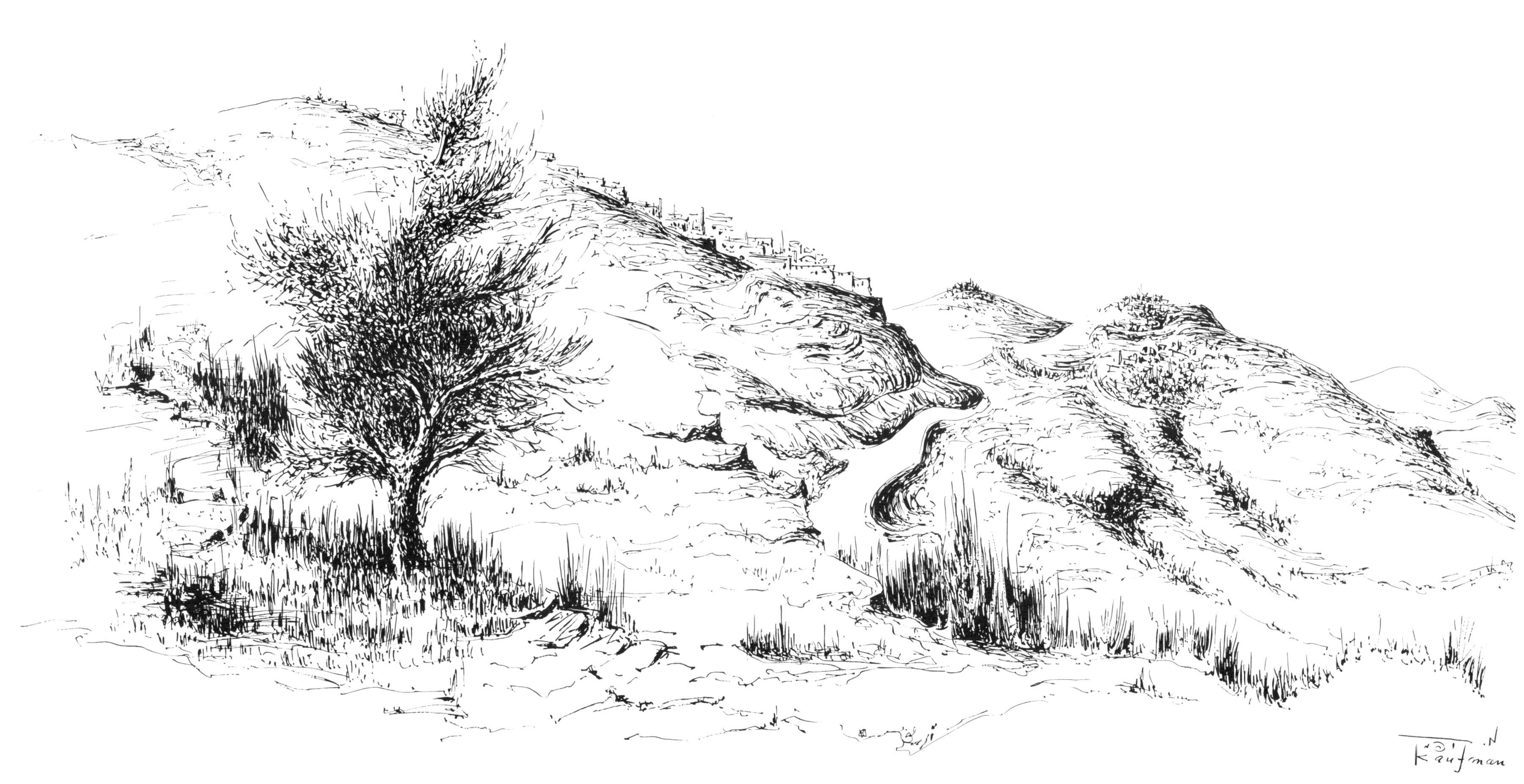
Kaufman

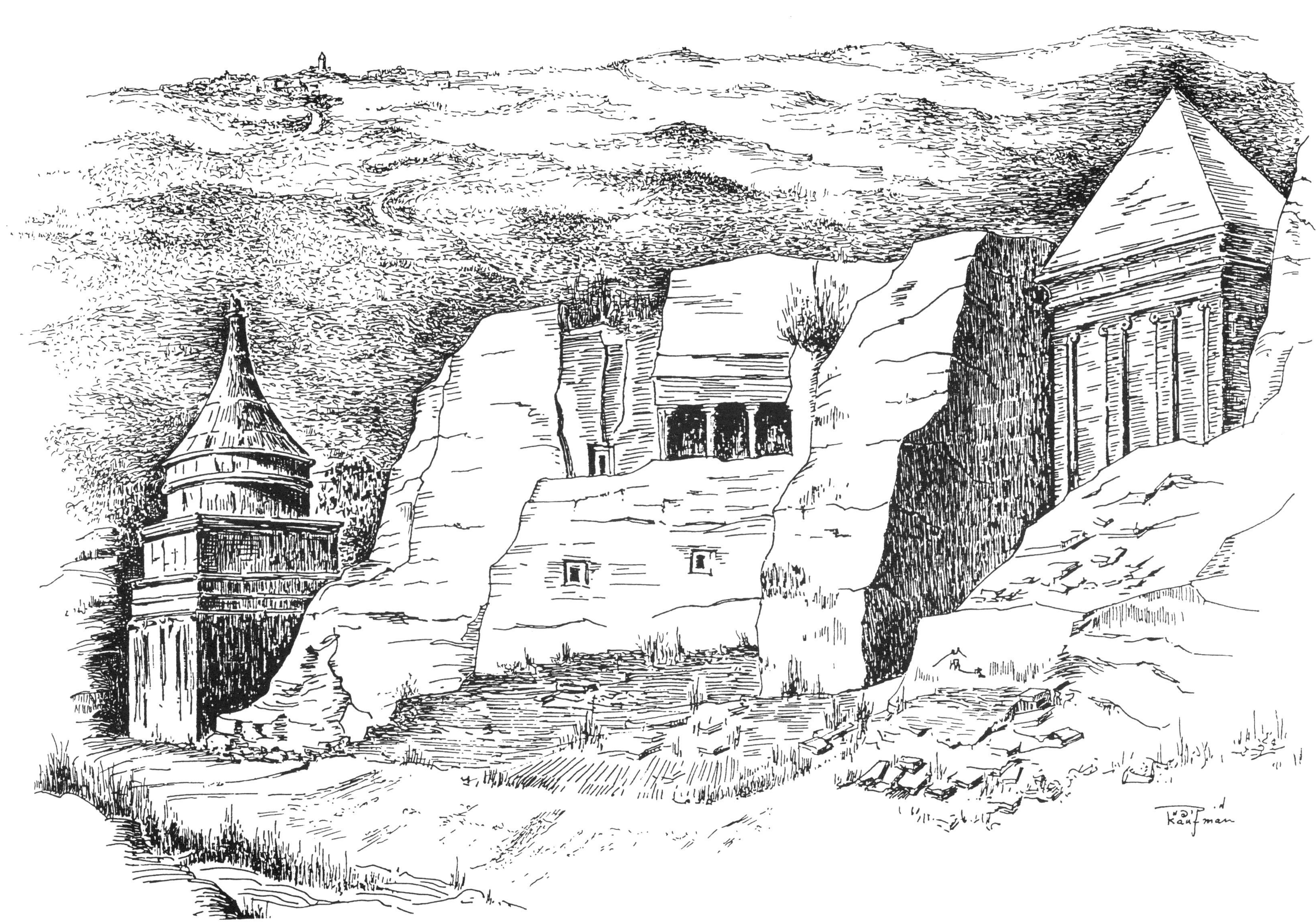
Kaufman

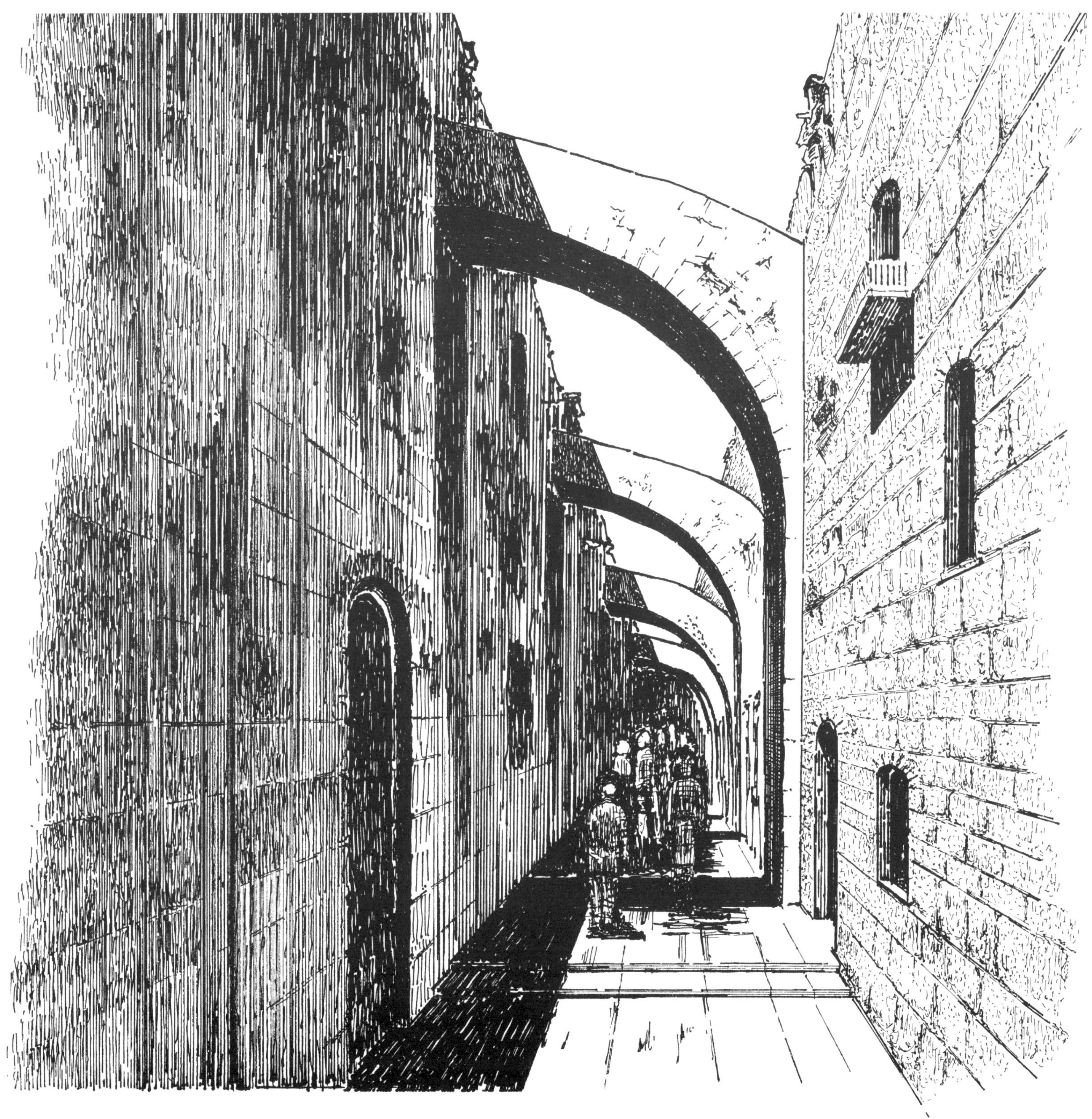

JUDEA AND SAMARIA

LIST OF LANDSCAPES

PAGE

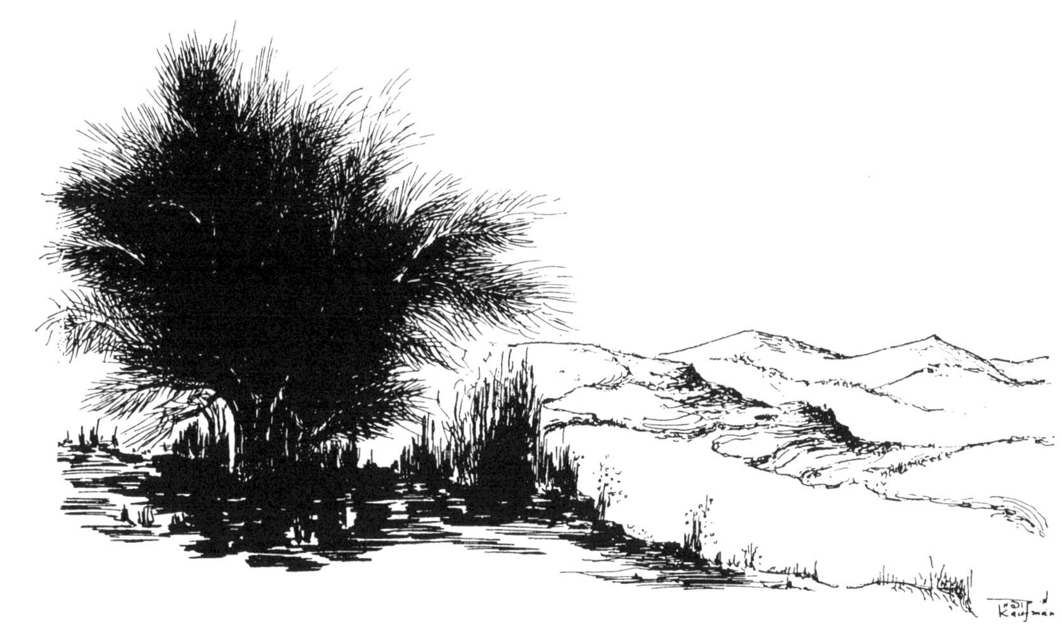

NAMES AND PLACES

Judea , known as the "Kingdom of Judah", was located south of Jerusalem and west of the Jordan River. Judea included the cities: Jerusalem, Hebron and Bethlehem. Under Roman rule it was called “Judea”.

“AND ELISHA SAID…WERE IT NOT THAT I REGARD THE PRESENCE OF JEHOSHAPHAT THE KING OF JUDAH, I WOULD NOT LOOK TOWARD THEE…”

(2ND KINGS Chapter 3 : 14)

“AND THE MEN OF JUDAH CAME, AND THERE THEY APOINTED DAVID KING OVER THE HOUSE OF JUDAH.”

(2nd SAMUEL Chapter 2 : 4)

Samaria is the region north of Jerusalem and in the central part of Israel. The ancient capital of this region was the city of Shechem.

“ AND HE BOUGHT THE HILL SAMARIA OF SHEMER FOR TWO TALENTS OF SILVER, AND BUILT ON THE HILL, AND CALLED THE NAME OF THE CITY WHICH HE BUILT’ AFTER THE NAME OF SHEMER, OWNER OF THE HILL, SAMARIA.”

(1ST KINGS Chapter 16 : 24)

“NOW JEHORAM THE SON OF AHAB BEGAN TO REIGN OVER ISRAEL IN SAMARIA THE EIGHTEENTH YEAR OF JEHOSHAPHAT KING OF JUDAH…”

(2ND KINGS Chpter 3 : 1)

St. George Monastery - located in the picturesque Wadi Qelt, between Jerusalem and Jericho. The Monastery is carved out of the rock and clings impressivly to the canyon walls. The Monastery was founded in the fifth century but was destroyed during the Persian invation. In the year 1179 it was restored again by the Crusaders. The present monastery was rebuilt around 1900 by the Greek Orthodox Church.

Hebron, one of the most ancient cities, is located south-west of Jerusalem on the main road to Beersheba. The Bible tells that Abraham made his home near Hebron and upon the death of his wife Sarah, he purchased a burial cave that today is known as the Tomb of the Patriarchs in Hebron.

“AND AFTER THIS, ABRAHAM BURIED SARAH HIS WIFE IN THE CAVE OF THE FIELD OF MACHPELAH BEFOR MAMRE: THE SAME IN LAND OF CANAAN.”

(GENESIS chapter 23:17)

“ THE DAYS THAT DAVID REIGNED OVER ISRAEL WERE FORTY YEARS; SEVEN YEARS REIGNED HE IN HEBRON AND THIRTY THREE YEARS IN JERUSALEM.”

(1ST KINGS chapter 2 :11)

The Jordan River flows from the height of Mount Hermon to the depth of the Dead Sea. The river forms part of the international boundry between Israel and the Kingdom of Jordan and is mentioned in the Bible 175 times. Jesus was baptized by John the Baptist in the Jordan River.

" AND THOSE TWELVE STONES, WHICH THEY TOOK OUT OF JORDAN, DID JOSHUA PITCH IN GILGAL. AND HE SPOKE UNTO THE CHILDREN OF ISRAEL SAYING ….LET YOUR CHILDREN KNOW “ISRAEL CAME OVER THIS JORDAN…”

(JOSHUA chapter 4 : 20-22)

“AND FIFTY MEN OF THE SONS OF THE PROPHETS WENT AND STOOD TO AFAR OFF: AND THEY STOOD BY JORDAN.”

(2ND KINGSchapter2:7)

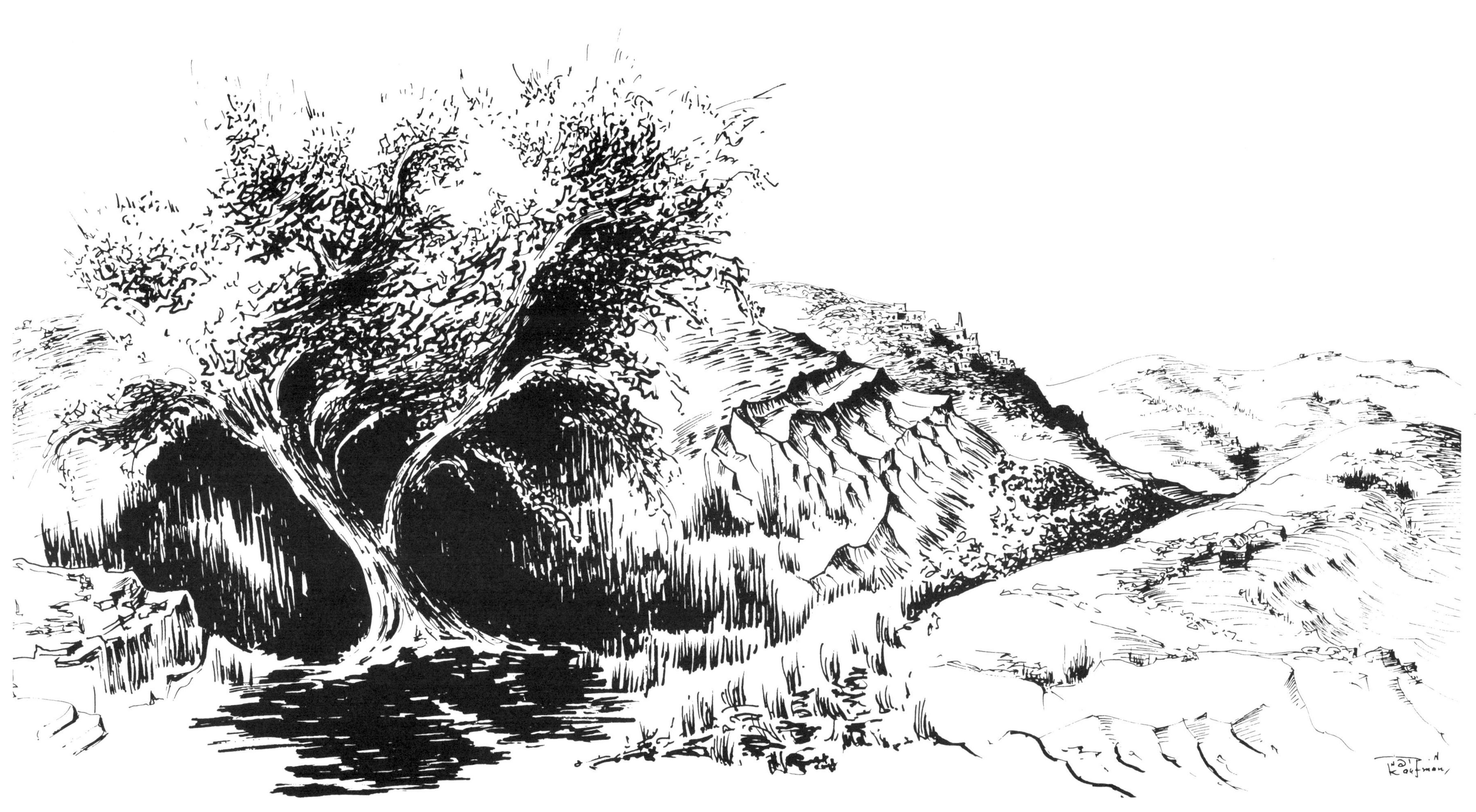

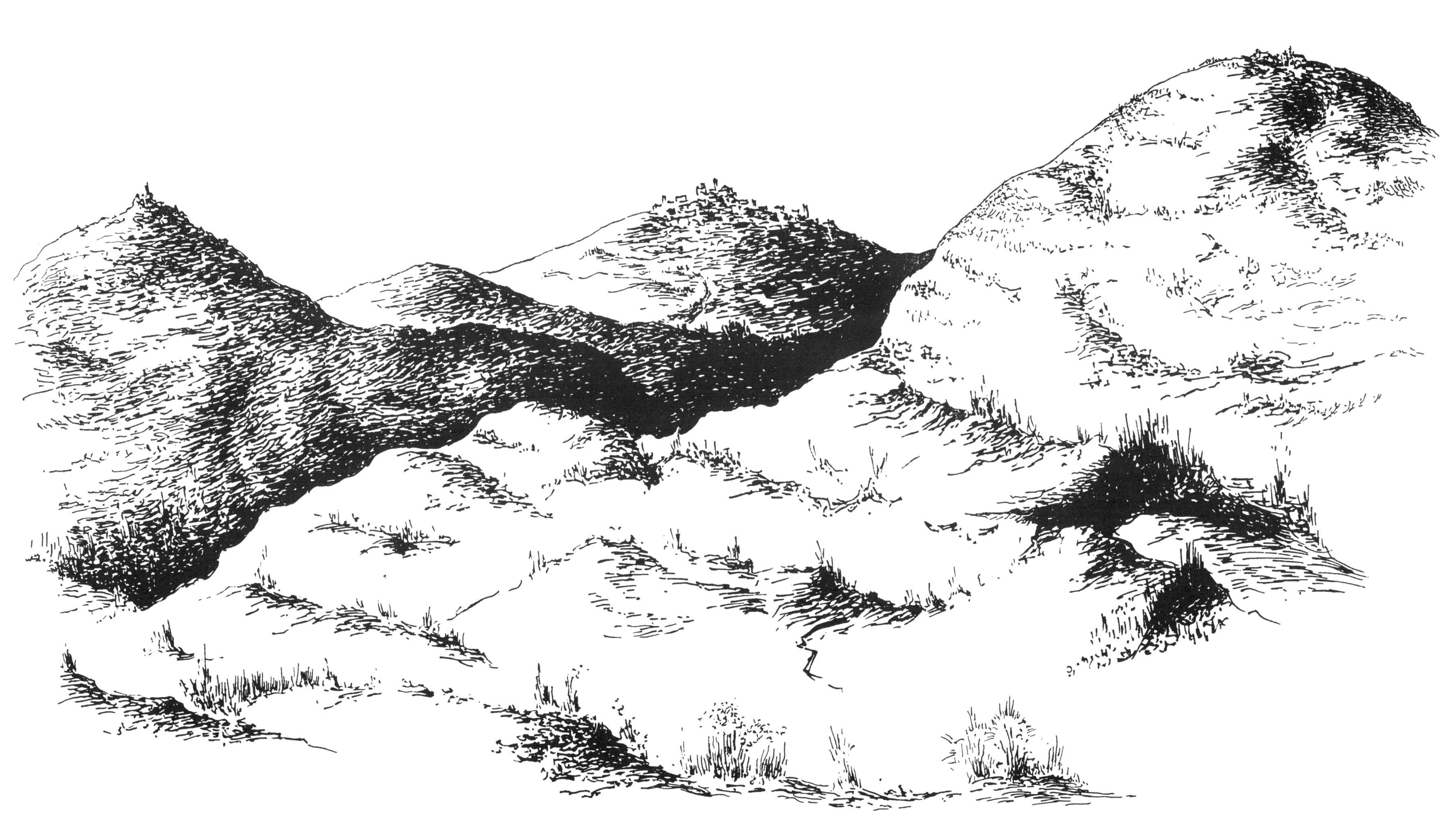

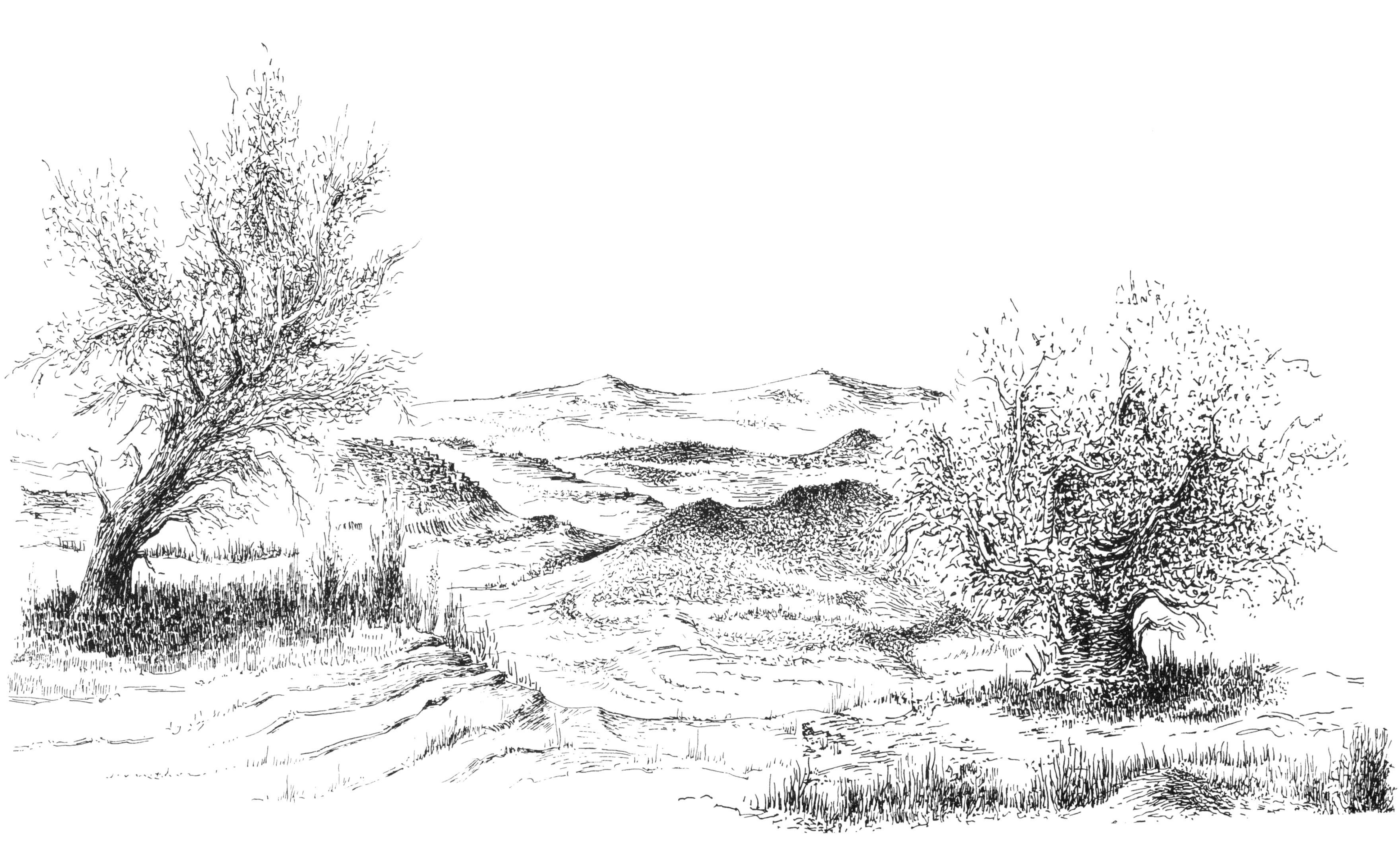

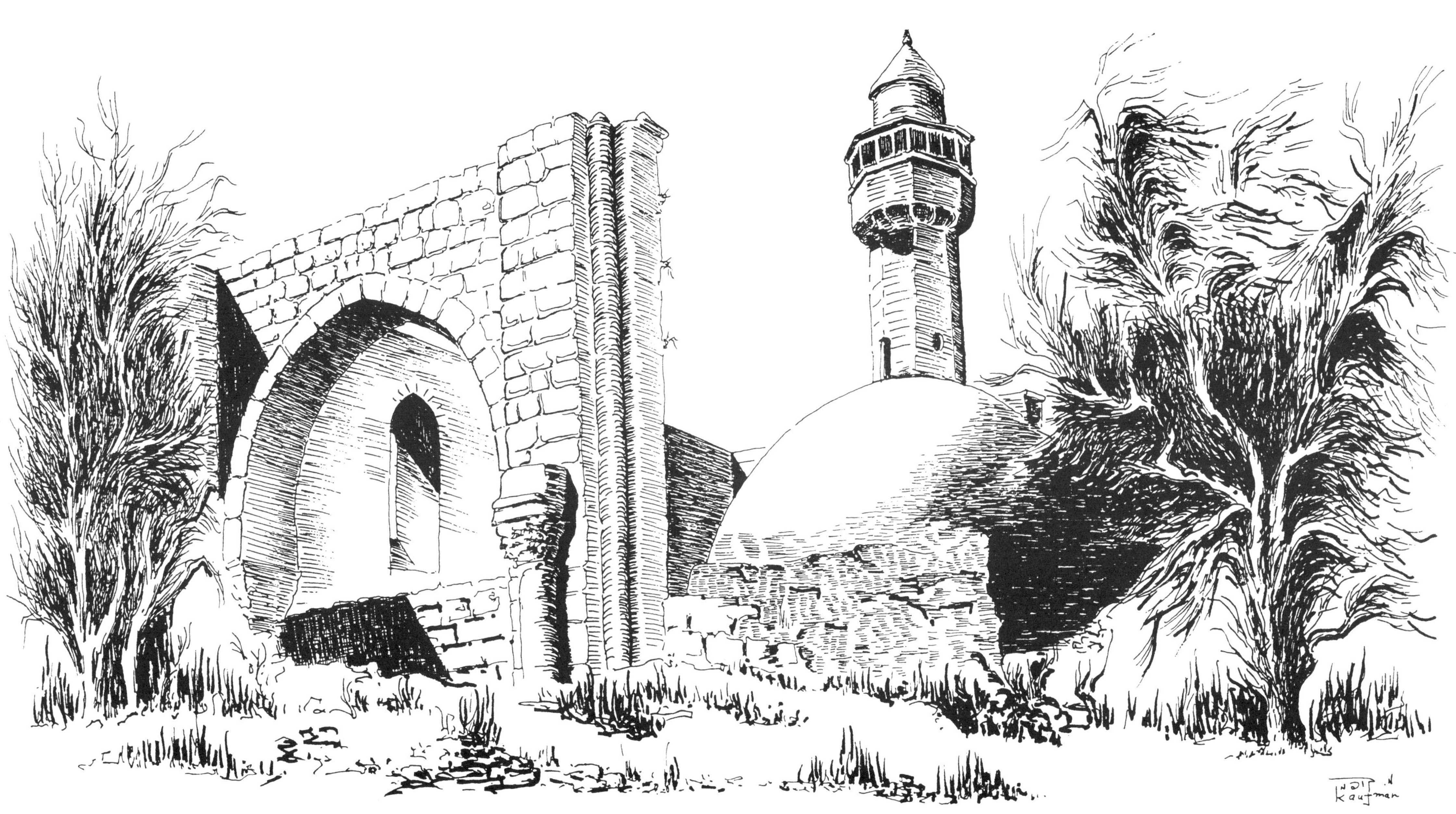
מ. קופמן
Kaufman

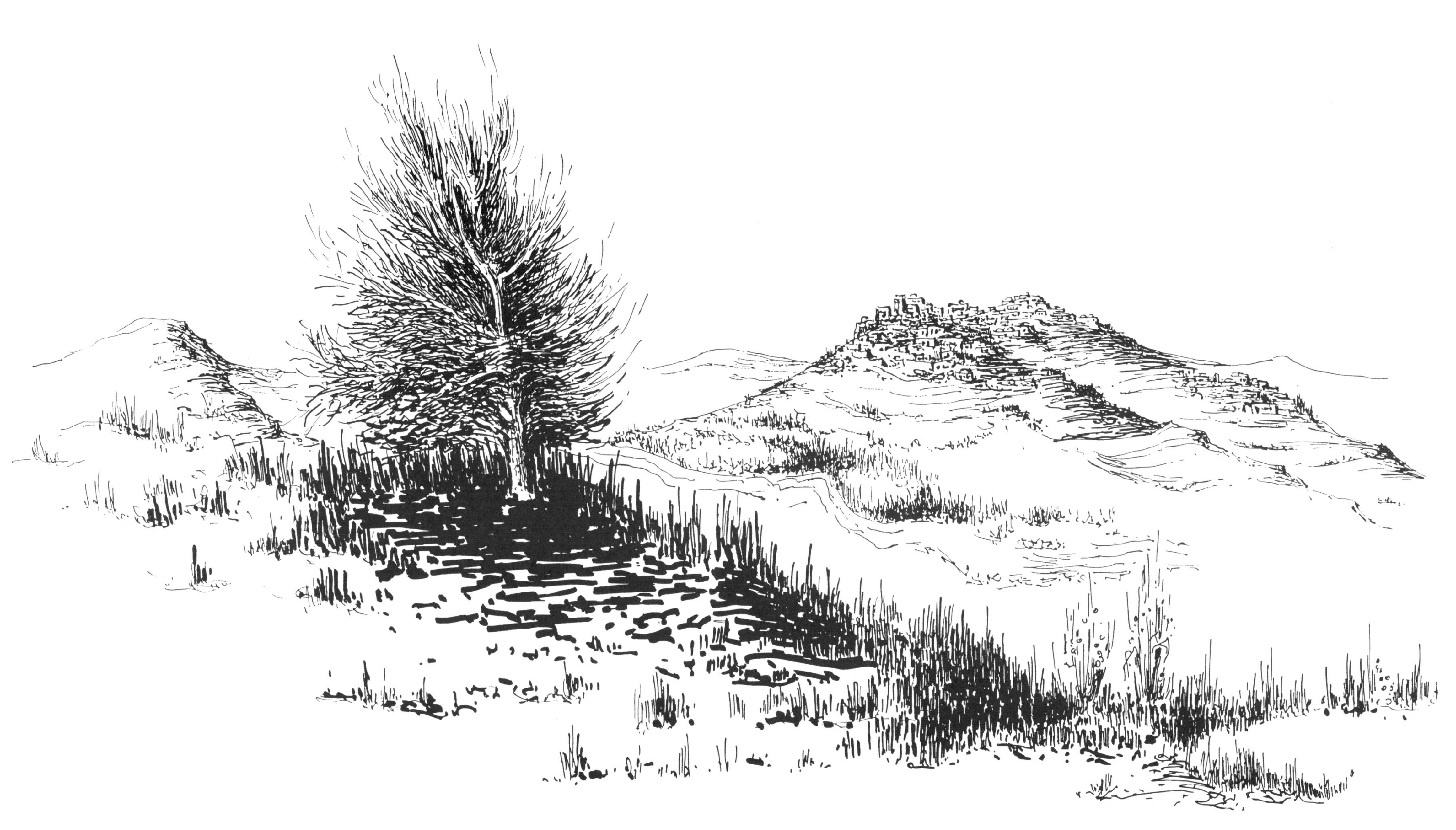

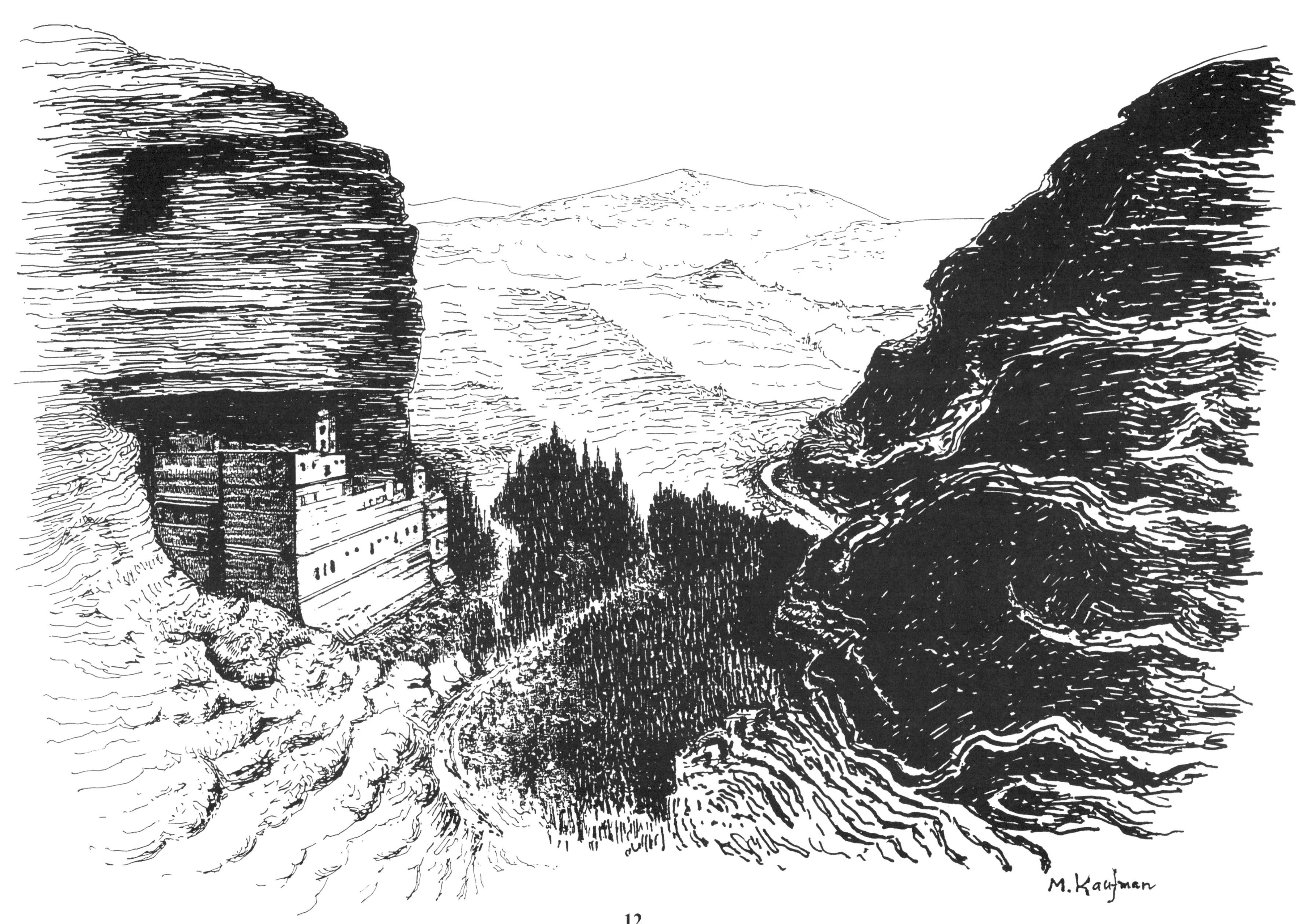
M. Kaufman

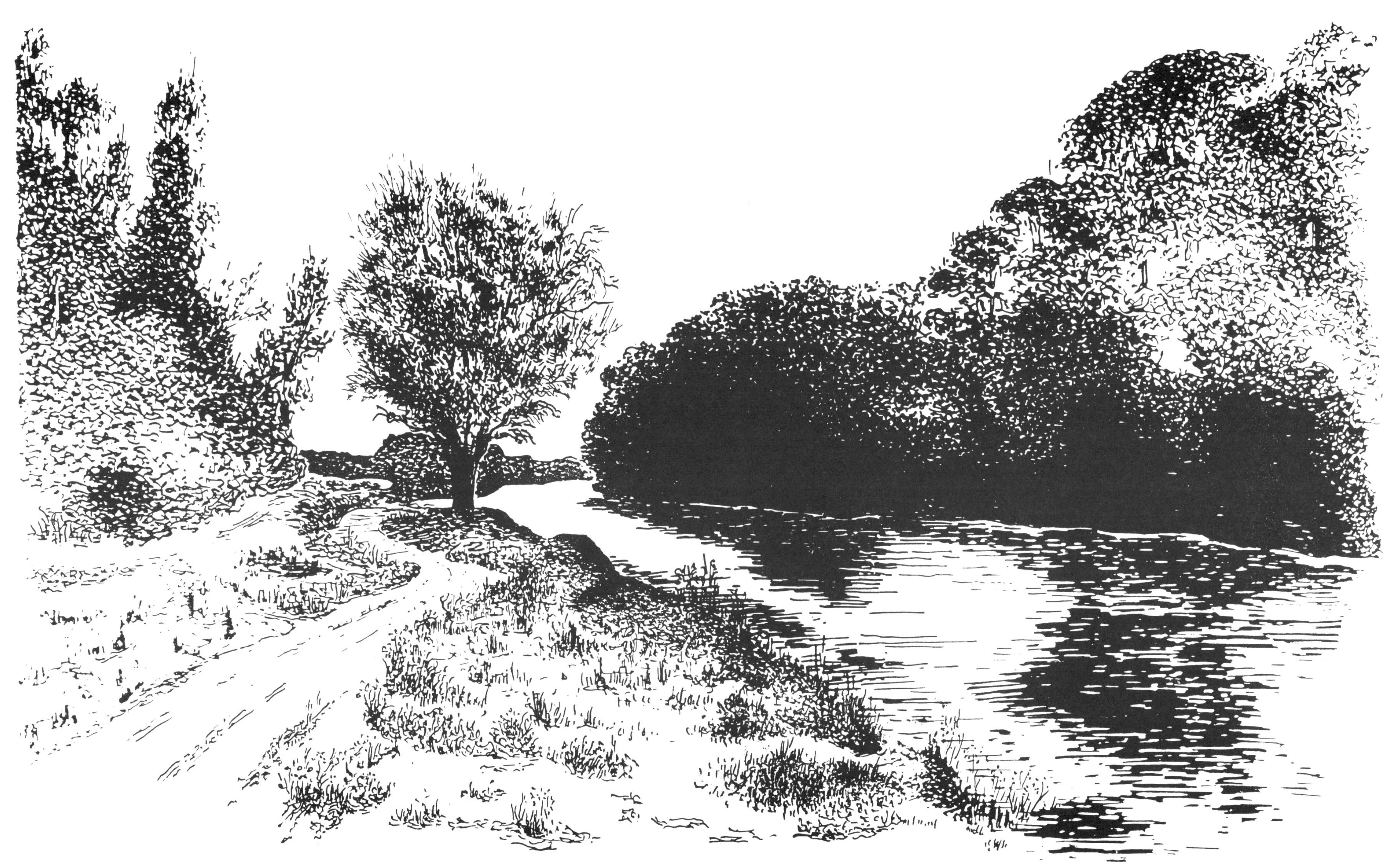

THE GALILEE

LIST OF LANDSCAPES

PAGE

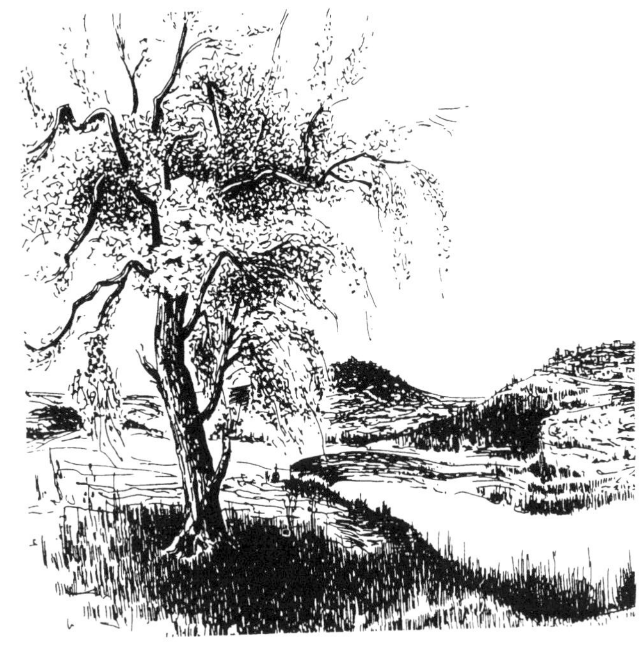

NAMES AND PLACES

Nazareth is one of the most important Christian holy sites in thc world. But in the period of Jesus Nazareth was a small and insignificant village. Nazareth is holy to Christians because of the events in Jesus's life that took place in Nazareth as described in the New Testament:
the annunciation of his birth, his childhood and his early manhood. In the city there are many churches and holy places: the modern Basilica of the Annunciation, the sisters of Nazareth convent, the Anglican church, Mary's well, the Salesian church of Jesus and many others.

The Galilee is Israel's northern region. It is generally mountainous and is devided geographically into Upper Galilee in the north and Lower Galilee in the south. In the region exist many holy sites of great significance to Judaism and Christianity.

The sea of Galilee - the beautiful "**sea of Kinnereth**" is located in the Galilee and is surrounded by the city of Tiberias on the west, by kibutz Ein-gev on the east and by many holy Christian places like : Bethsaida, Tabgha, Magdala and Capernaum "the home of Jesus" 2000 years ago.

" HIS KINGDOM INCLUDED THE EASTERN ARABAH FROM THE SEA OF KINNERETH TO THE SEA OF ARABAH...." (JOSHUA chapter 12 : 3)

The Dan River in the Upper Galilee is the main source of the Jordan River.

Mount Arbel - a prominent physical landmark around the Sea of Galilee located near the western shore in the vicinity of ancient Magdala, home of Mary Magdalene. Arbel is mentioned in the Bible only in Hosea 10:14

Zefat is the capital of the Galilee and considered one of the four Jewish "holy cities" in Israel. A montainous city, high above sea level, known for its being a center of Kabbalah and Jewish mysticism.

Hanita, once an anciant Jewish settlment on the northern border mentioned in the 2nd and 3rd century. Kibutz Hanita was established in 1938 at the northern border some 350 meters above sea level.

Acre – Akko a city and port on the bay of Haifa. It was captured by the Arabs in 638 A.D. In 1104 it was captured by the Crusaders and in 1187 was taken by Saladin. In the 3rd Crusades it was captured again and given to the Knights Hospitalers (Knights of St. John) and for the next century it was the center of the Christian possession in the Holy Land. Akko was taken by the Ottoman Turks in 1517. In 1799 the city withstood a 61 day sicgc by Napoleon. In 1918 it was captured by the British troops and in 1948 Akko was captured by the Israeli forces in the Arab – Israeli war. The city is a popular tourist site and includes an ancient citadel, walled fortifications and churches dating from the Crusades.

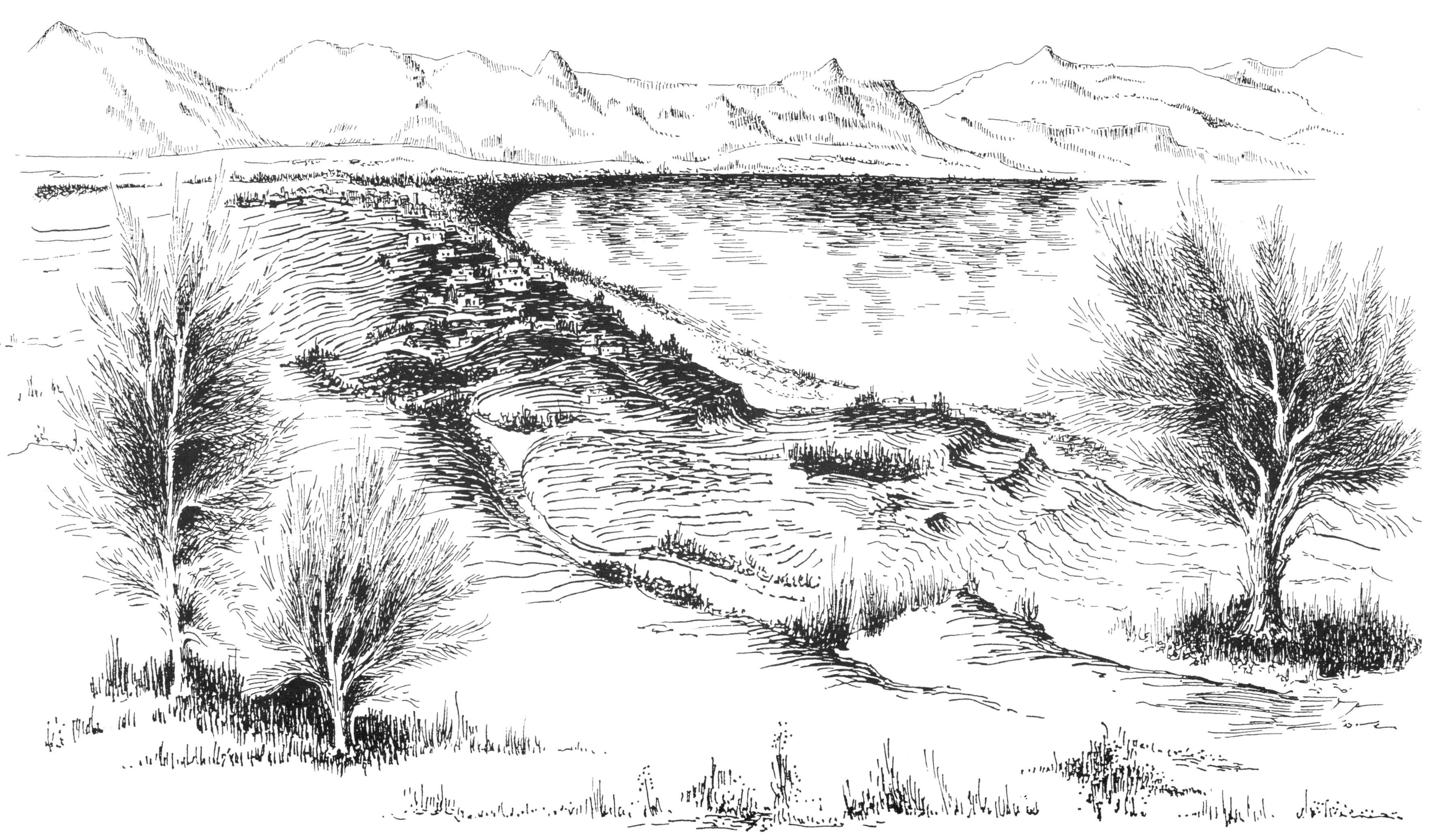

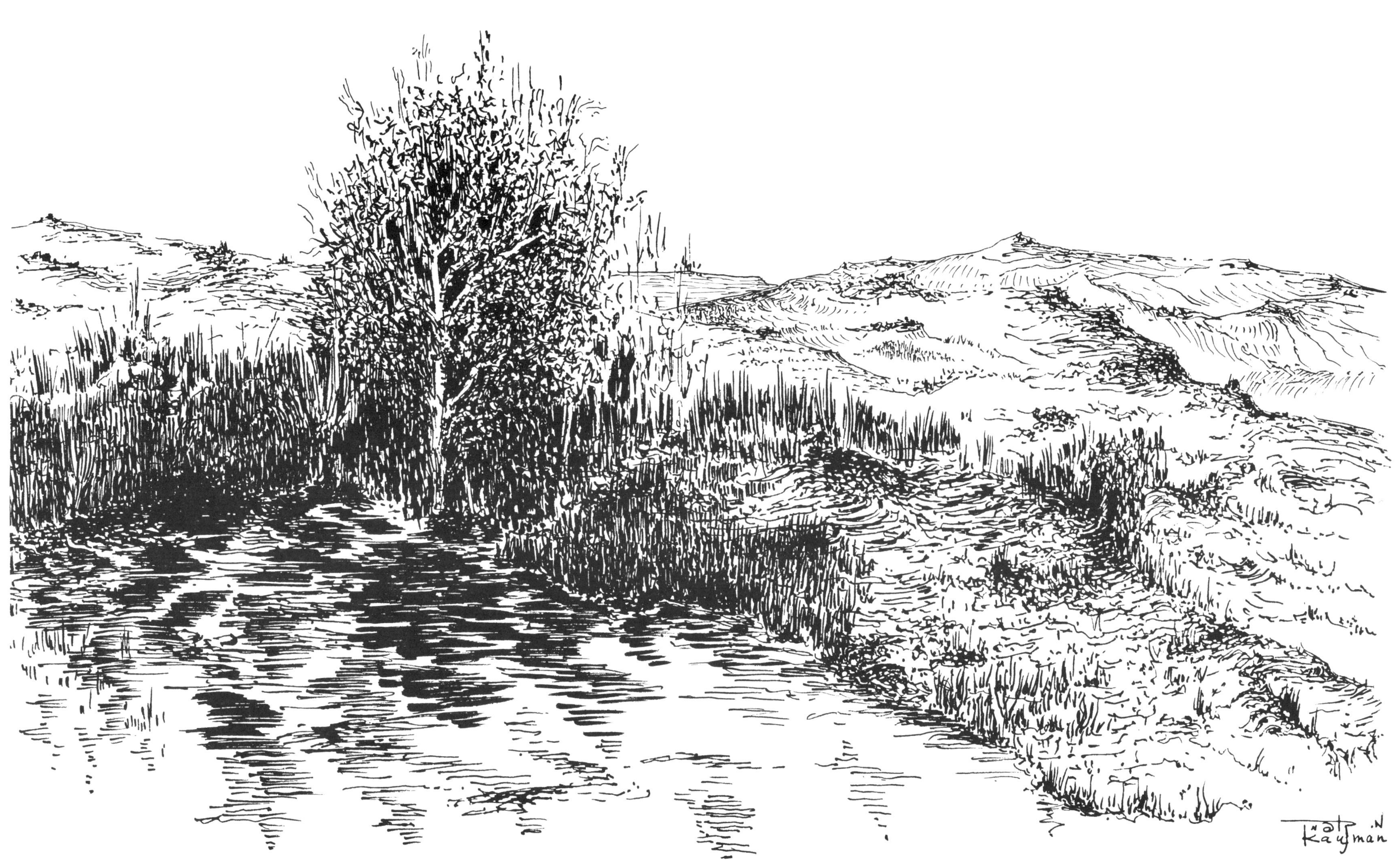
Kaufman

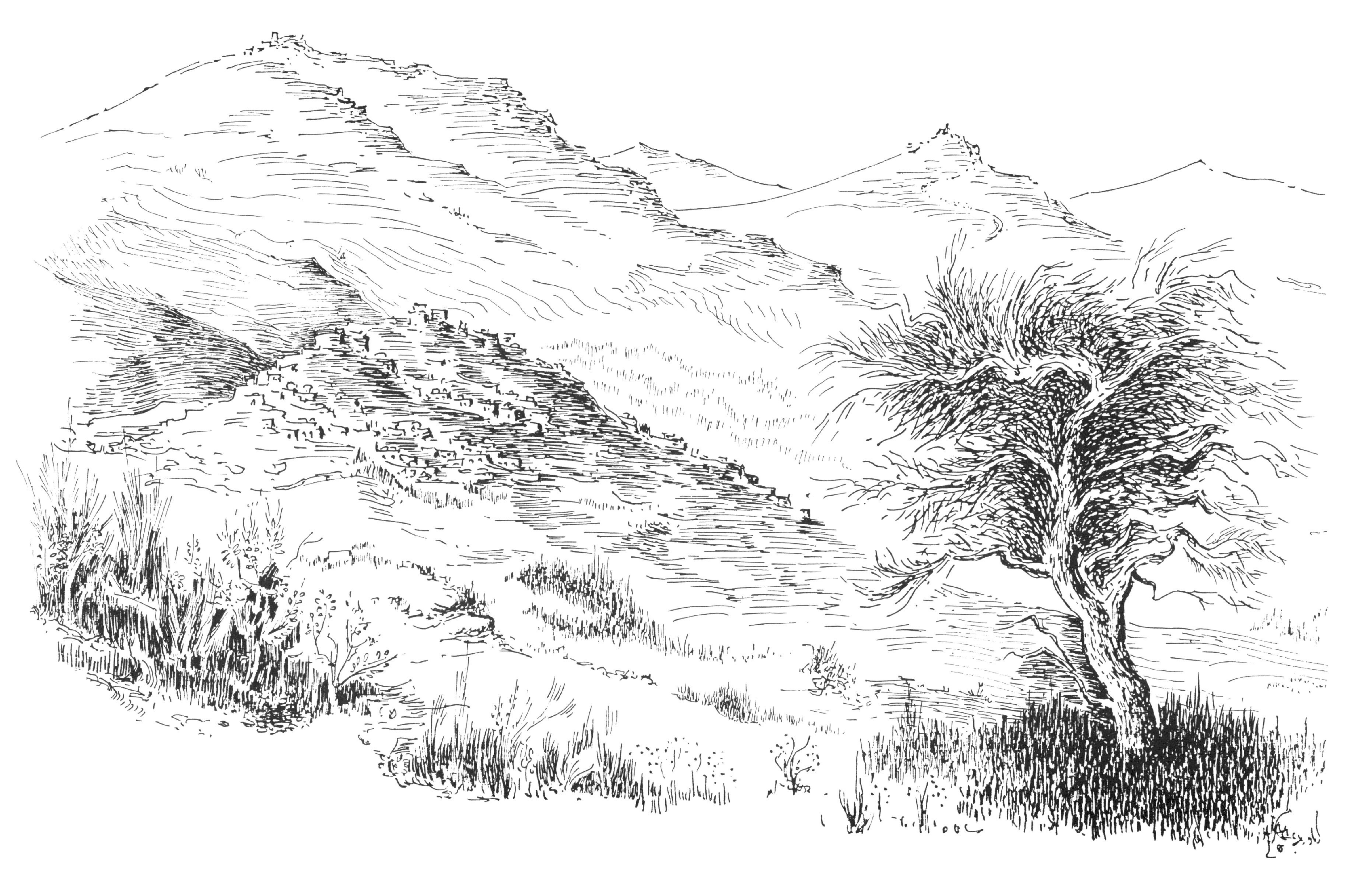

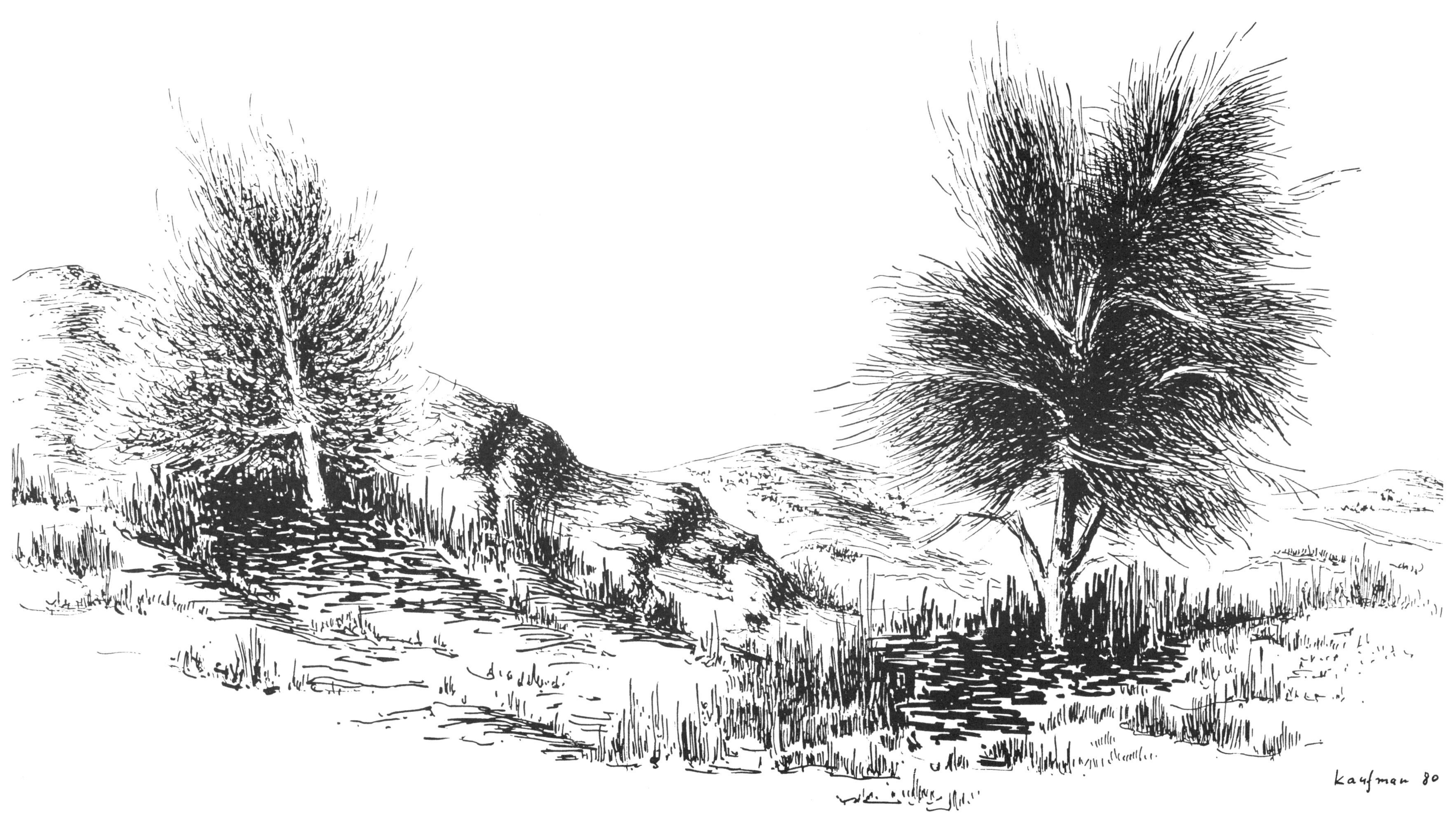
Kaufman 80

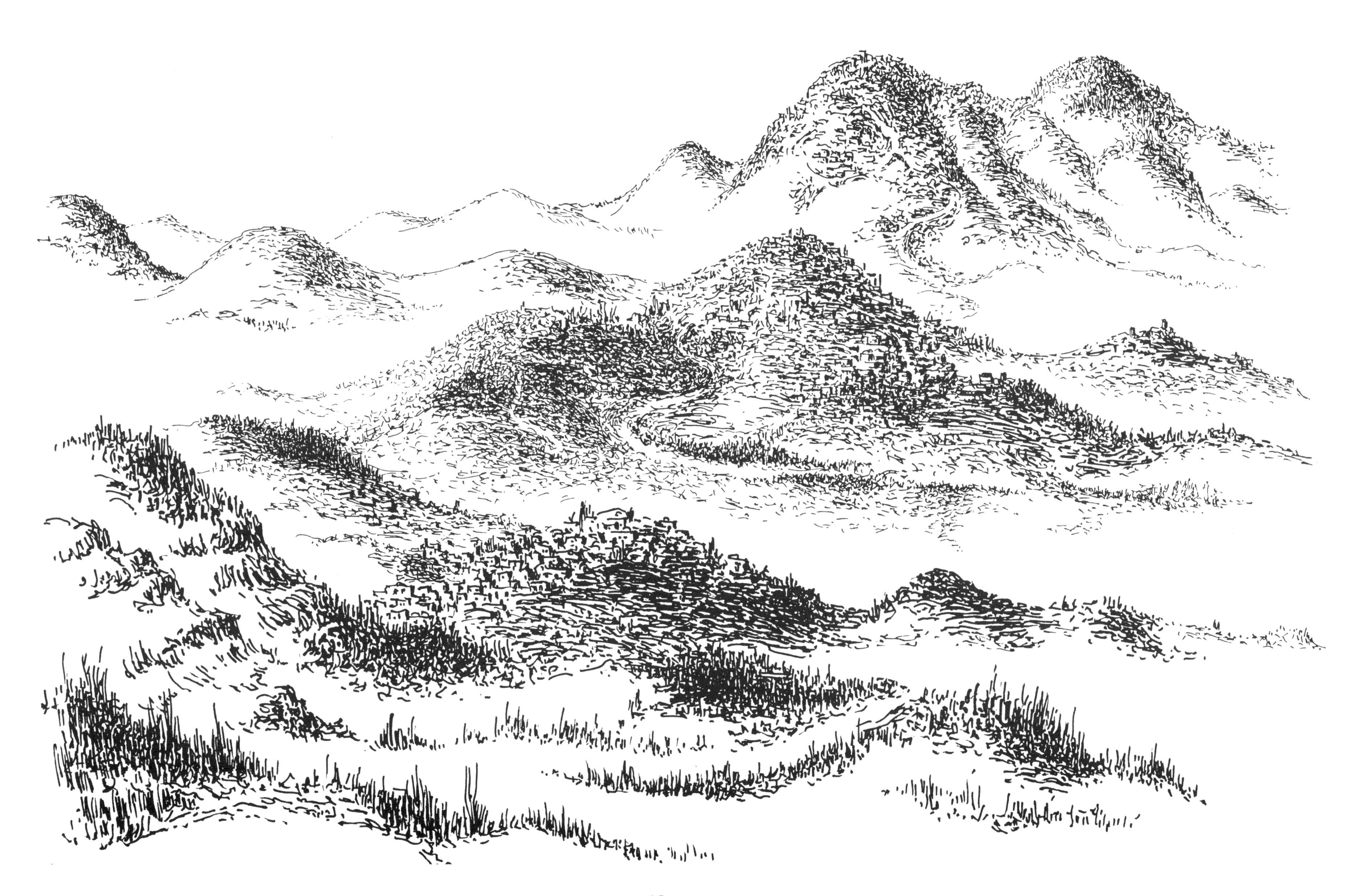

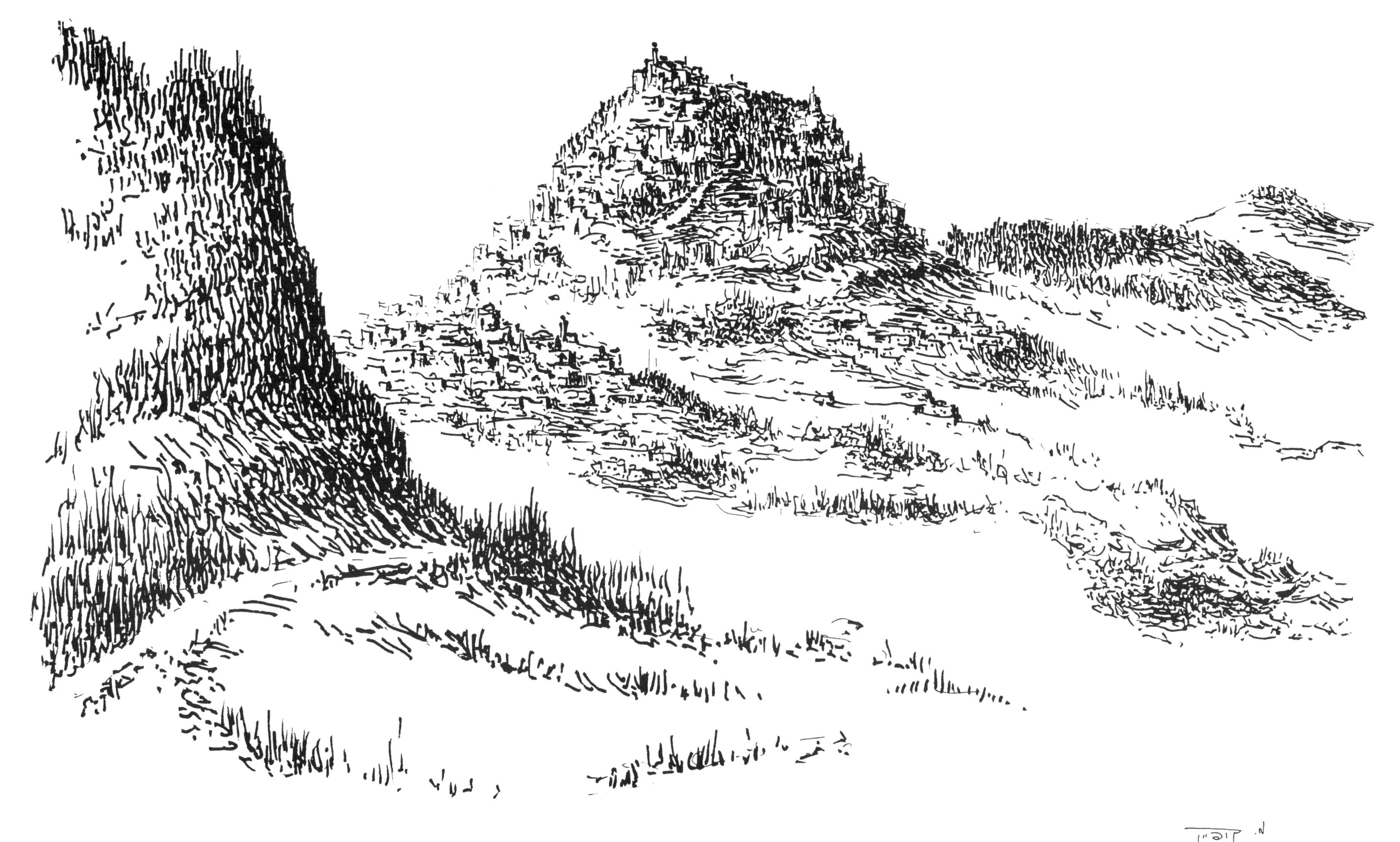
Kaufman

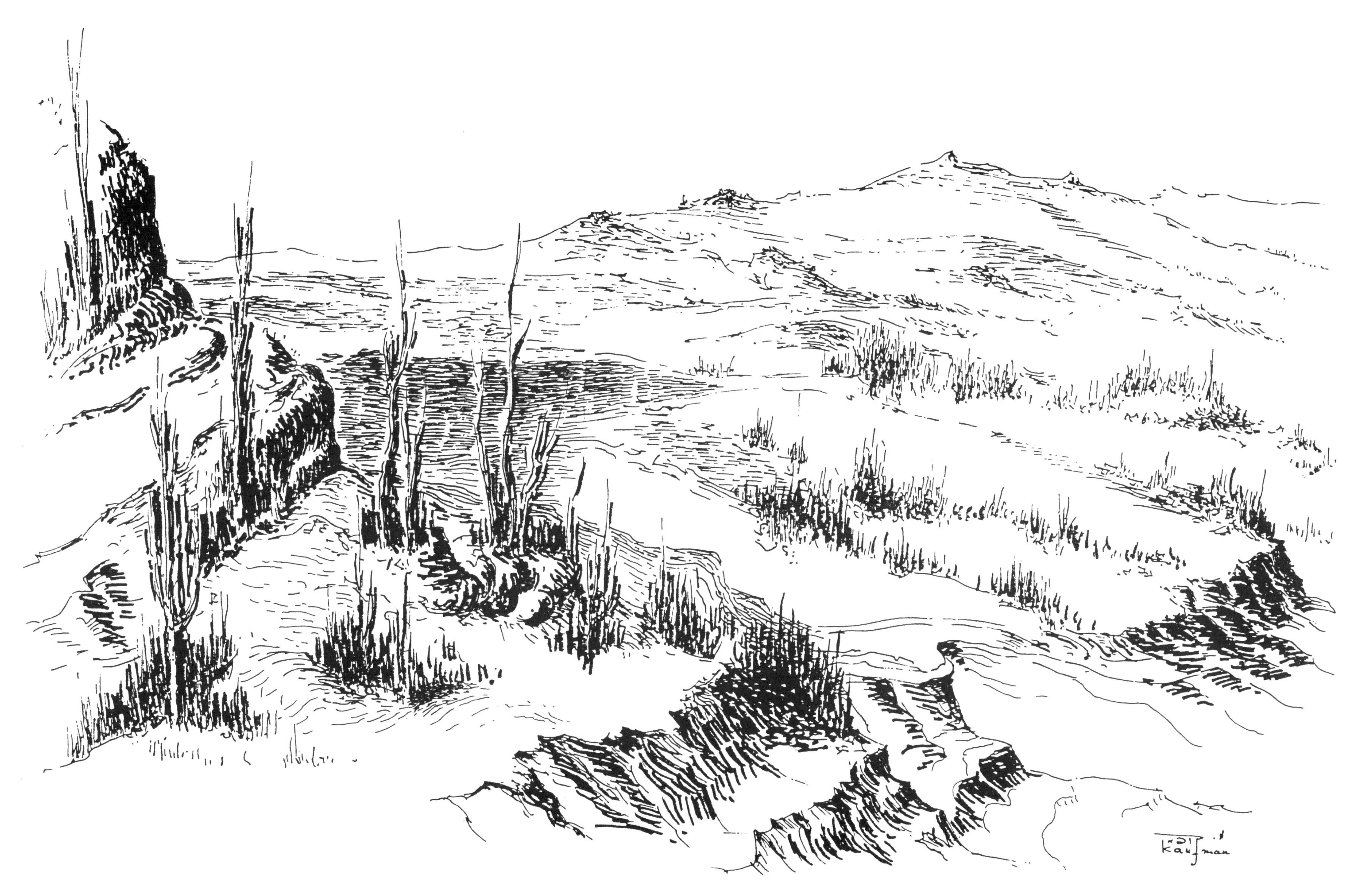
Kaufman

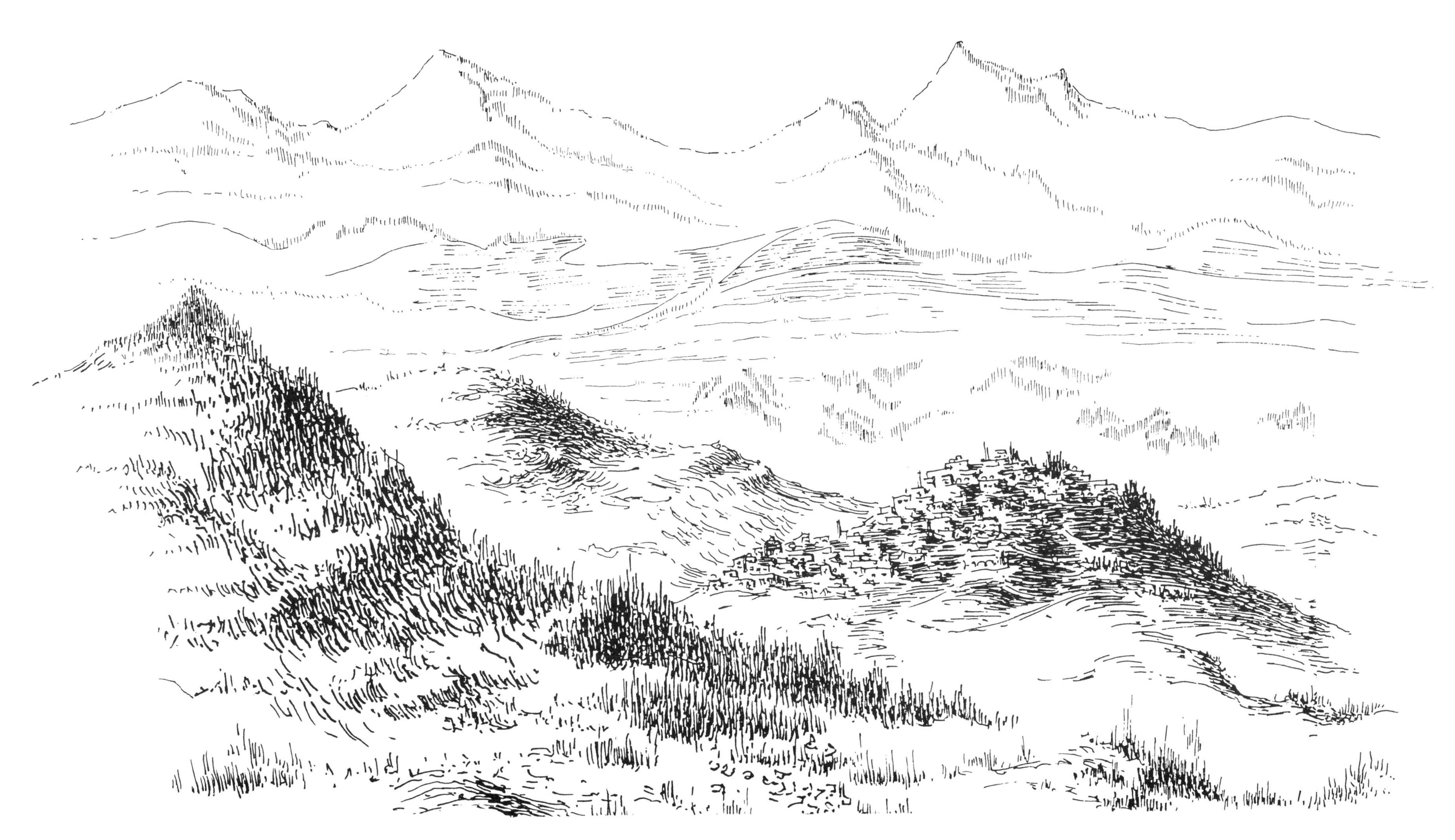

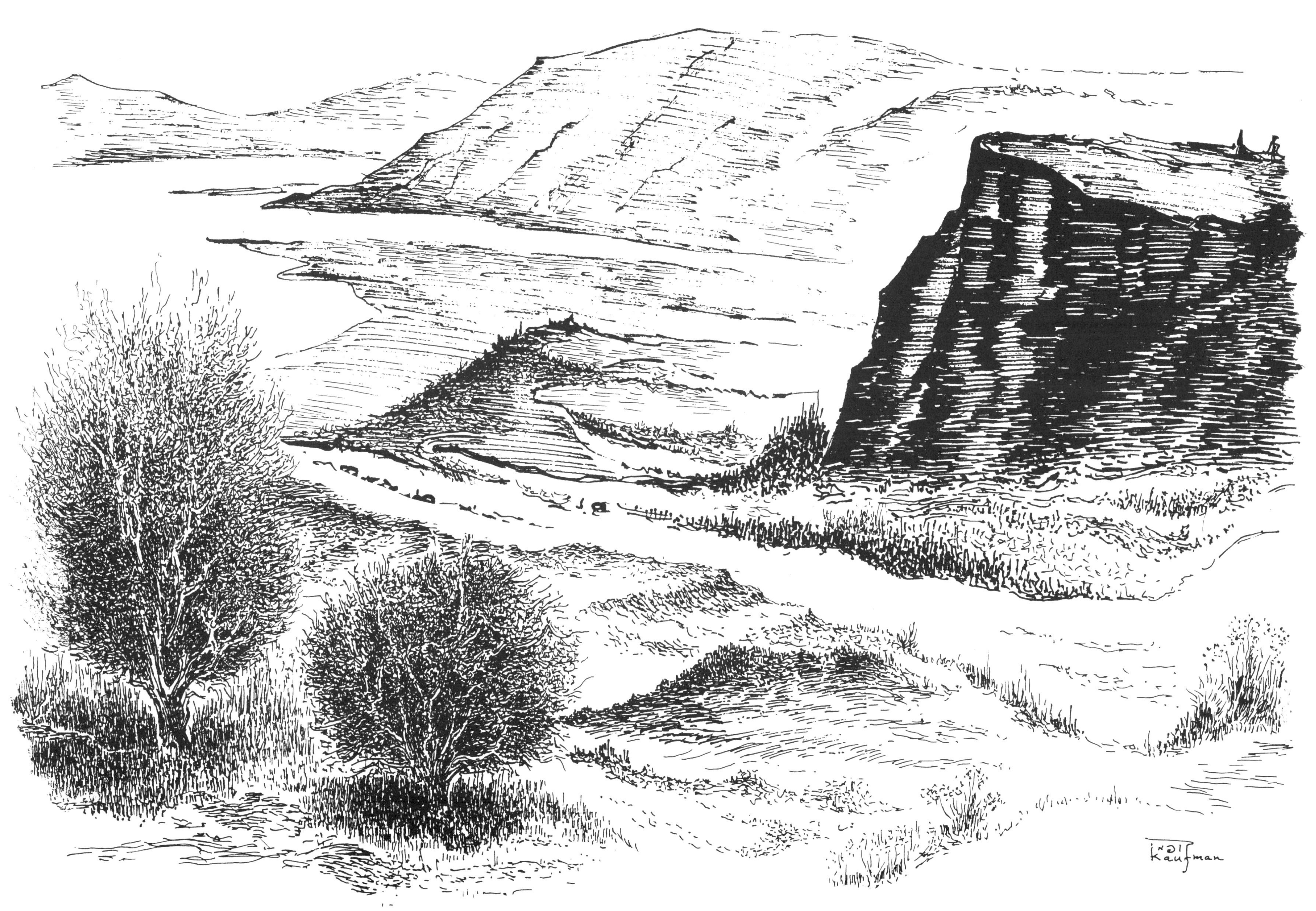
Kaufman

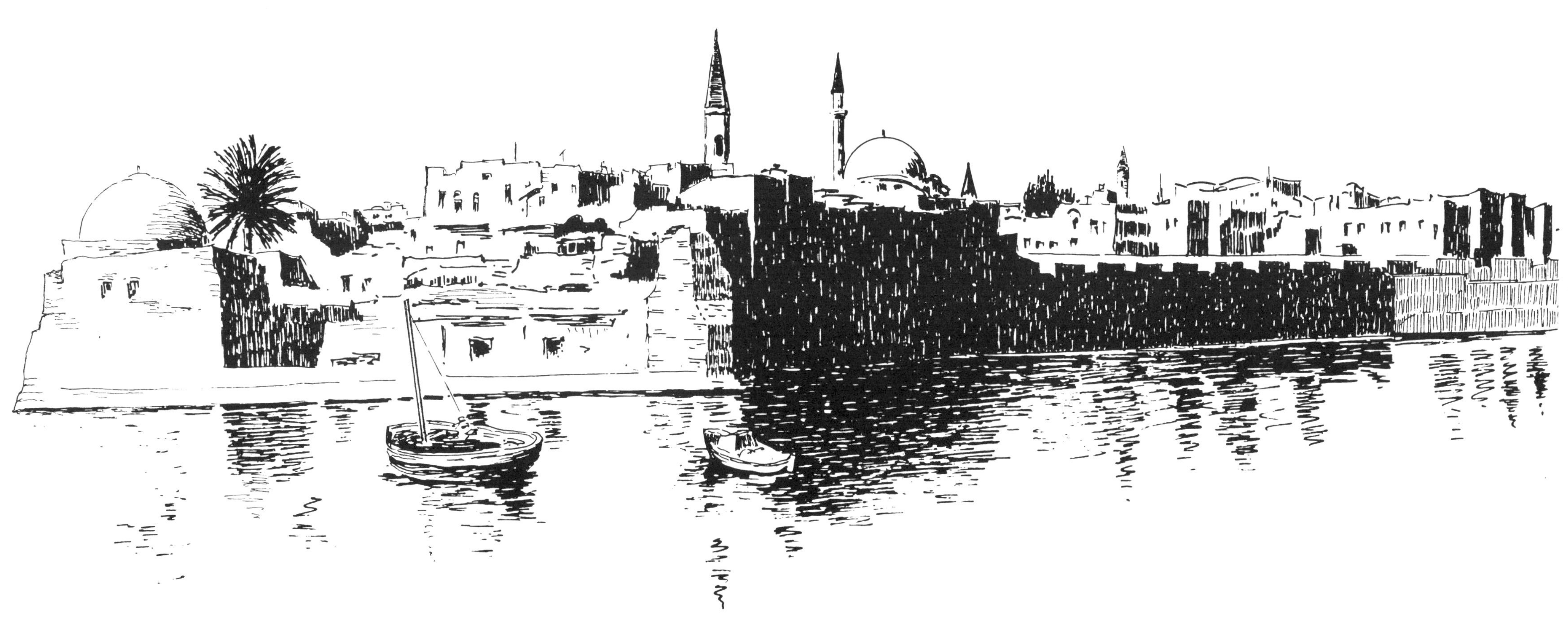

THE NEGEV AND SINAI

LIST OF LANDSCAPES

PAGE

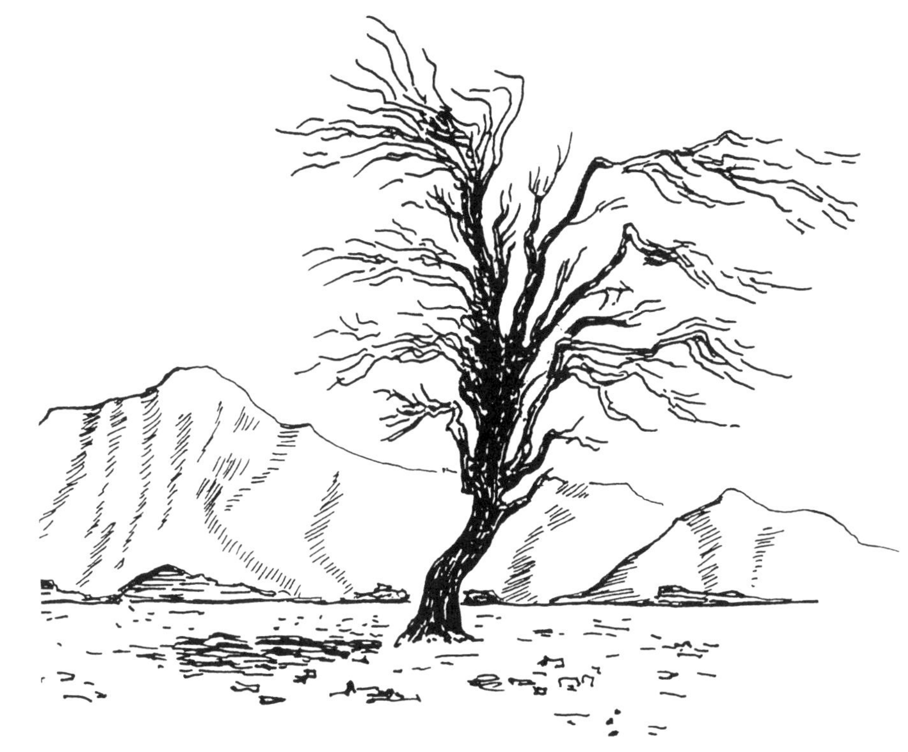

NAMES AND PLACES

The Dead Sea is a salt lake on the border between Israel and Jordan. The suface of the Dead Sea is about 400 m below sea level and is the lowest place on earth. Because of containing the saltiest water in the world the sea supports no life.
The ancient cities of Sodom and Gomorrah mentioned in the Bible were situated on the shore of the Dead Sea – "Salt Sea" in the Bible. Nowadays, the Dead Sea coast is a site of hotels, spas and recreation.

"THEN THE LORD RAINED UPON SODOM AND GOMORRAH BRIMSTONE AND FIRE FROM THE LORD OUT OF HEAVEN. AND HE OVERTHREW THOSE CITIES, AND ALL THE PLAIN, AND ALL THE INHABITANTS OF THE CITIES, AND THAT WHICH GREW UPON THE GROUND."

(GENESIS chapter 19 : 24,25)

"THESE CAME AS ALLIES TO THE VALLEY SIDDIM THAT IS THE SALT SEA"

(GENESIS chapter 14 :3)

Qumran is located on the barren terrace between the cliffs of the Judean desert and the Dead Sea. The famous Dead Sea Scrolls were found in the caves of Qumran sealed in clay jars. The scrolls contain manuscripts such as Isaiah that are part of the Bible.

The Aravah is the valley between the Dead Sea and the gulf of Eilat, along the border between Israel and the Kingdom of Jordan.

The Negev – the southern region of Israel. The northern part of the Negev is good sheep country. Its rolling hills surround large broad plains.The southern part of the Negev is the most arid region in Israel.

Eilat is mentioned in the Bible and called Eloth and Etzion Geber. An archeological expedition excavated the biblical site of Etzion Geber proving that it had been a fortified settlement from the 10th to the 4th century B.C. The Crusaders built naval garrisons in Elath but since then the only inhabitants of the region were nomadic bedouin tribes. On march 10, 1949 the Israel Defence Force began a 5 day campaign to reach Eilat, and on March 14 , 1949 the whole region was conquered by Israel ending the War of Independence.
In those days this region was desolate and the only structure there was a police station with some poor rooms known by the name "Um Rashrash". Nowadays, with the population of 50,000 residents the city of Eilat has become a leading tourist center, offering wide range of hotels, attractions, restaurants and all sorts of entertainments.

" AND KING SOLOMON MADE A NAVY OF SHIPS IN ETZION GEBER, WHICH IS BESIDE ELOTH, ON THE SHORE OF THE RED SEA, IN THE LAND OF EDOM"

(1ST KINGS chapter 9 : 26)

Mount sinai is the holy mount where, according to the Old Testament, Moses received the Ten Commandments from God.
The Mount is located in the wilderness of Sinai and draws pilgrims for over a thousand years. The Sinai peninsula is an Egyptian territory.

" AND MOUNT SINAI WAS ALTOGETHER ON A SMOKE, BECAUSE THE LORD DESCENDED UPON IT IN FIRE: AND THE SMOKE THEREOF ASCENDED AS THE SMOKE OF A FURNACE, AND THE WHOLE MOUNT QUAKED GREATLY."
" AND THE LORD CAME DOWN UPON MOUNT SINAI, ON THE TOP OF THE MOUNT: AND THE LORD CALLED MOSES UP TO THE TOP OF THE MOUNT; AND MOSES WENT UP. "

(EXODUS chapter 19 : 18, 20)

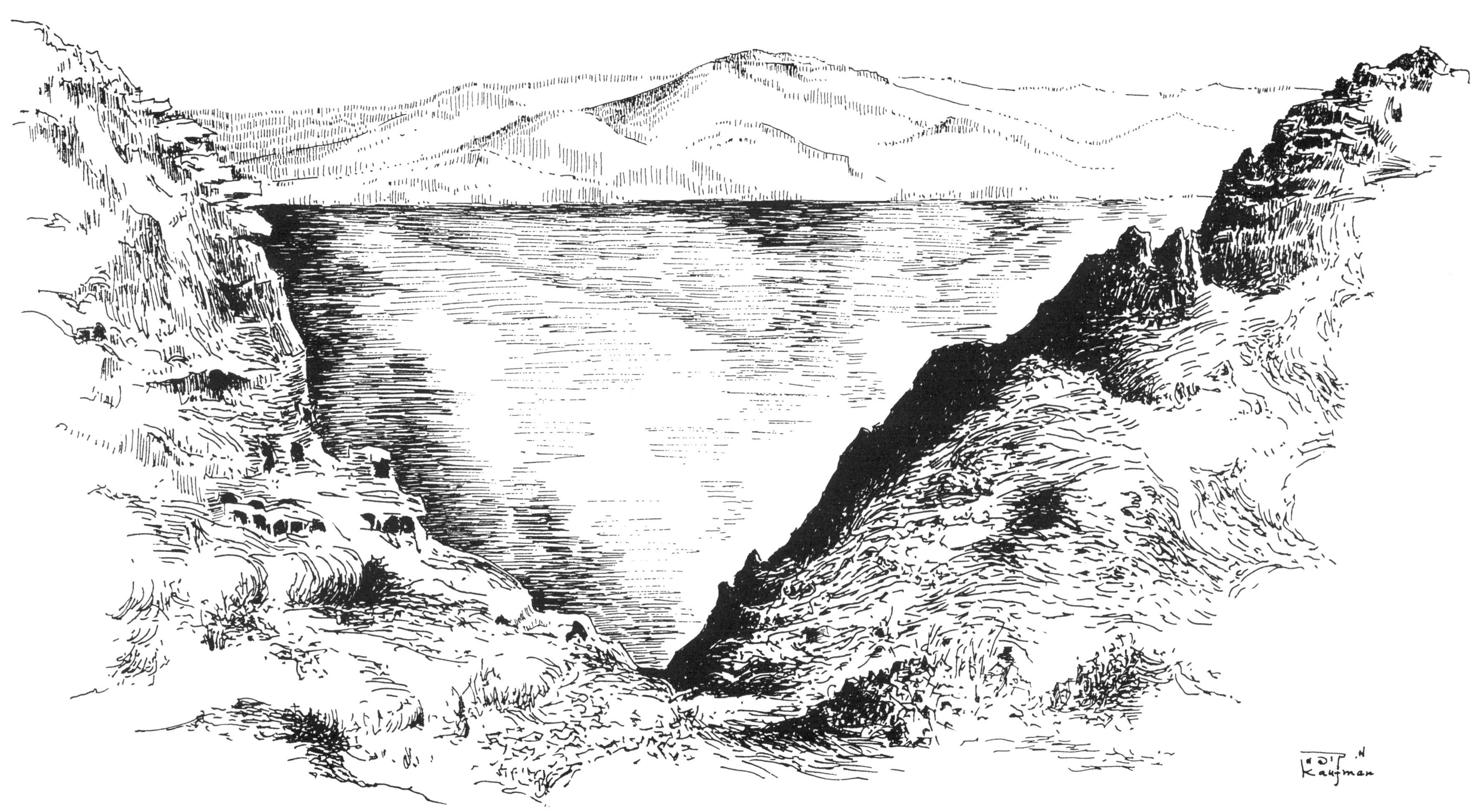
Kaufman

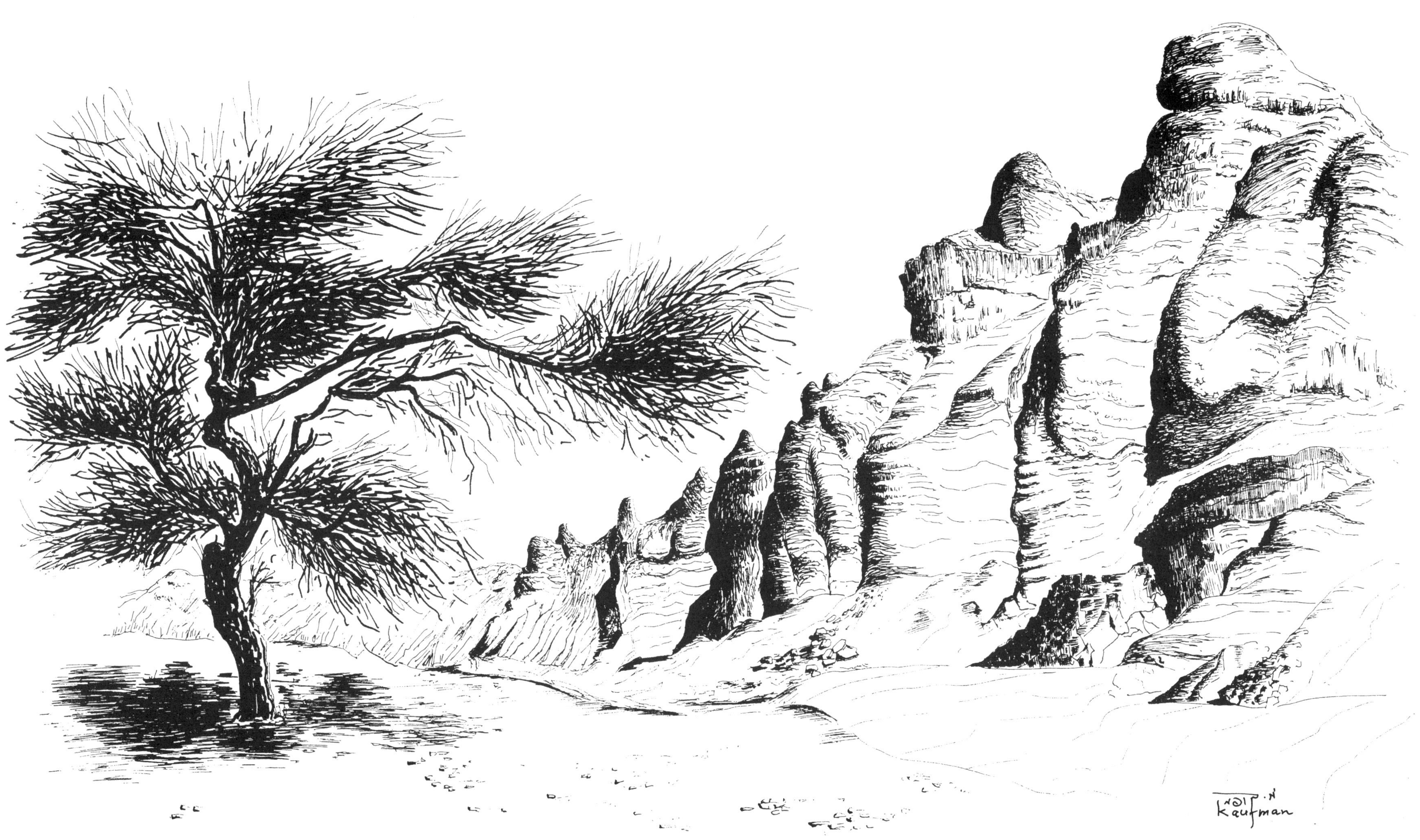
Kaufman

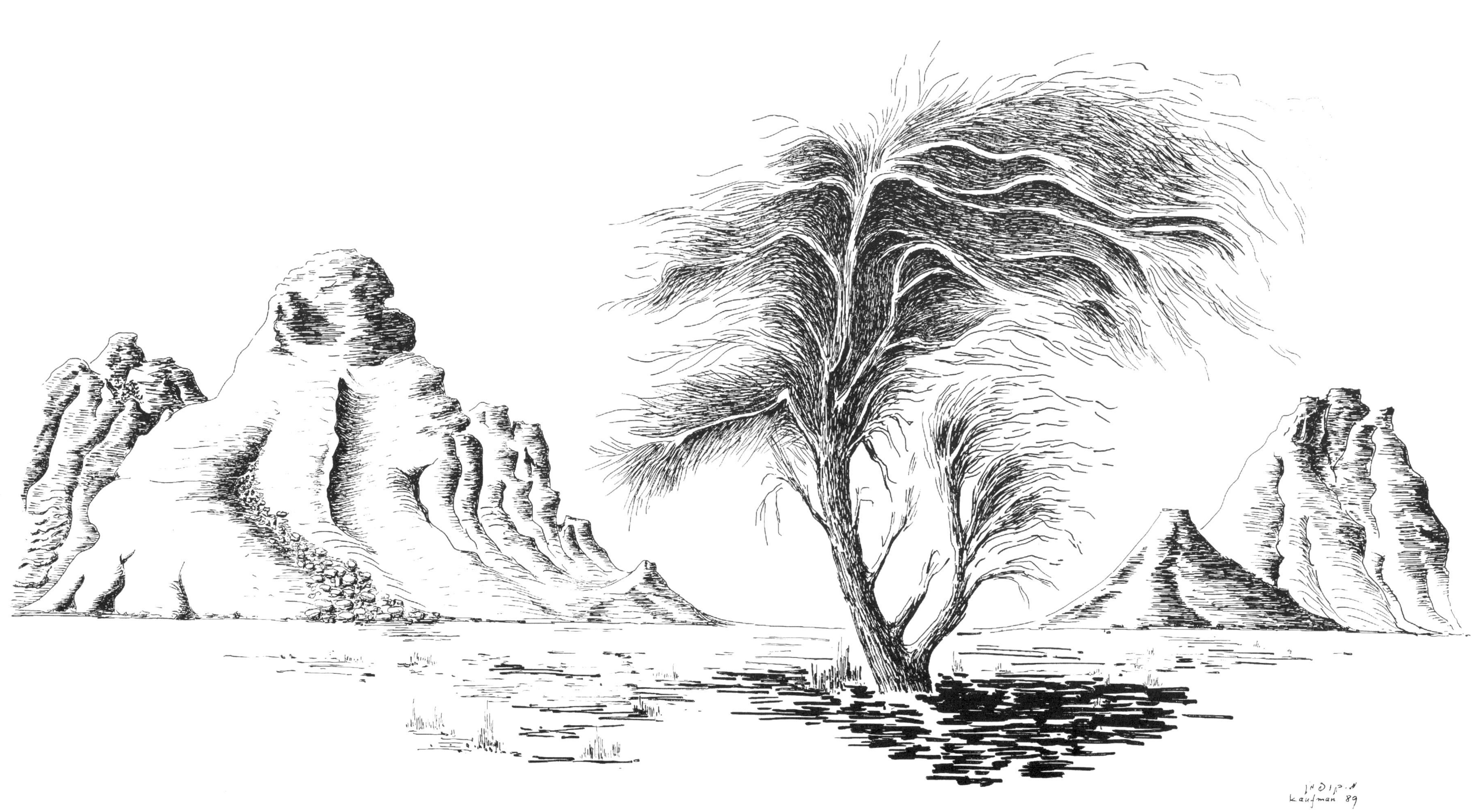
א. קופמן
kaufman 89

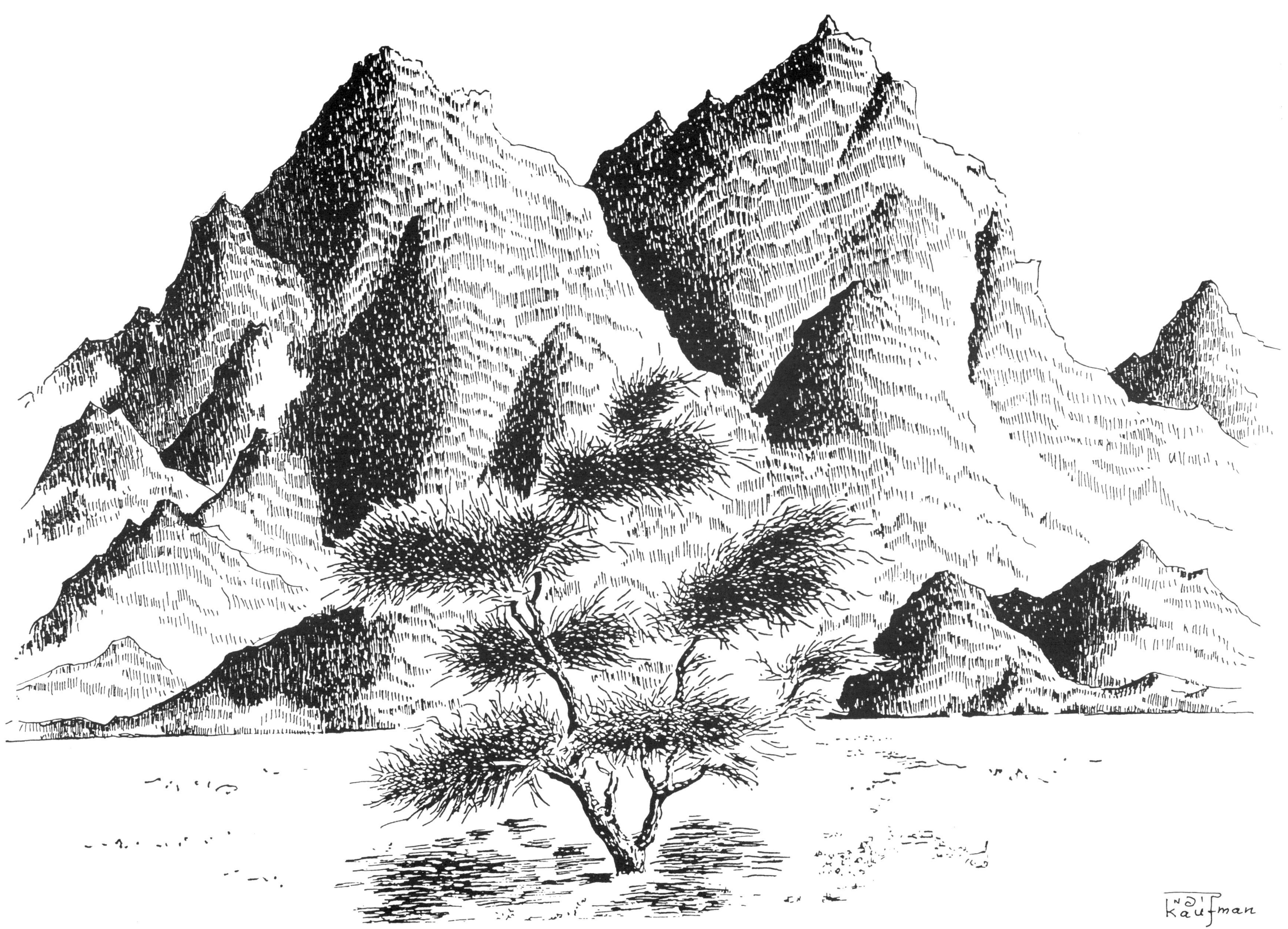
Kaufman

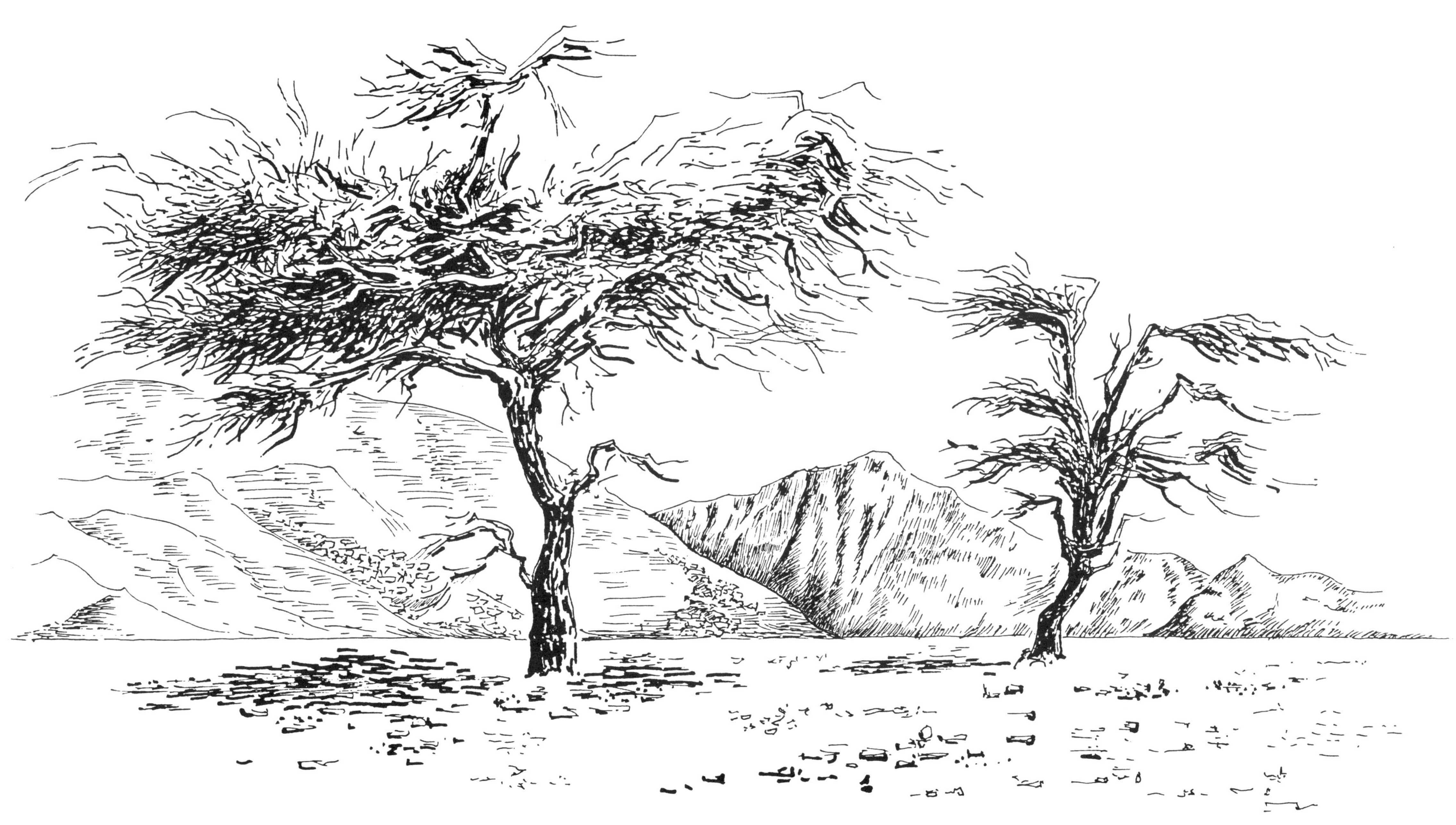
Kaufman

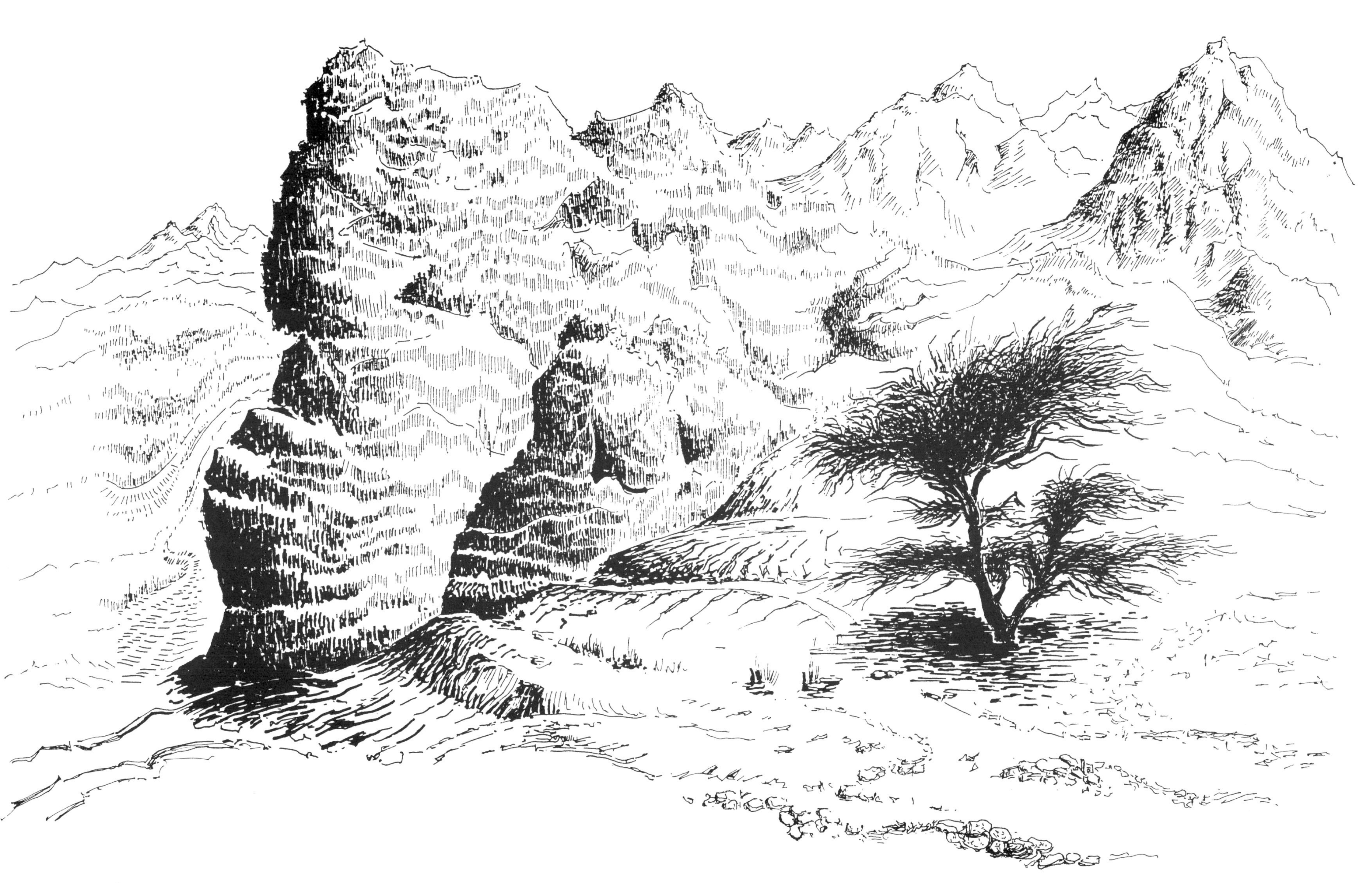

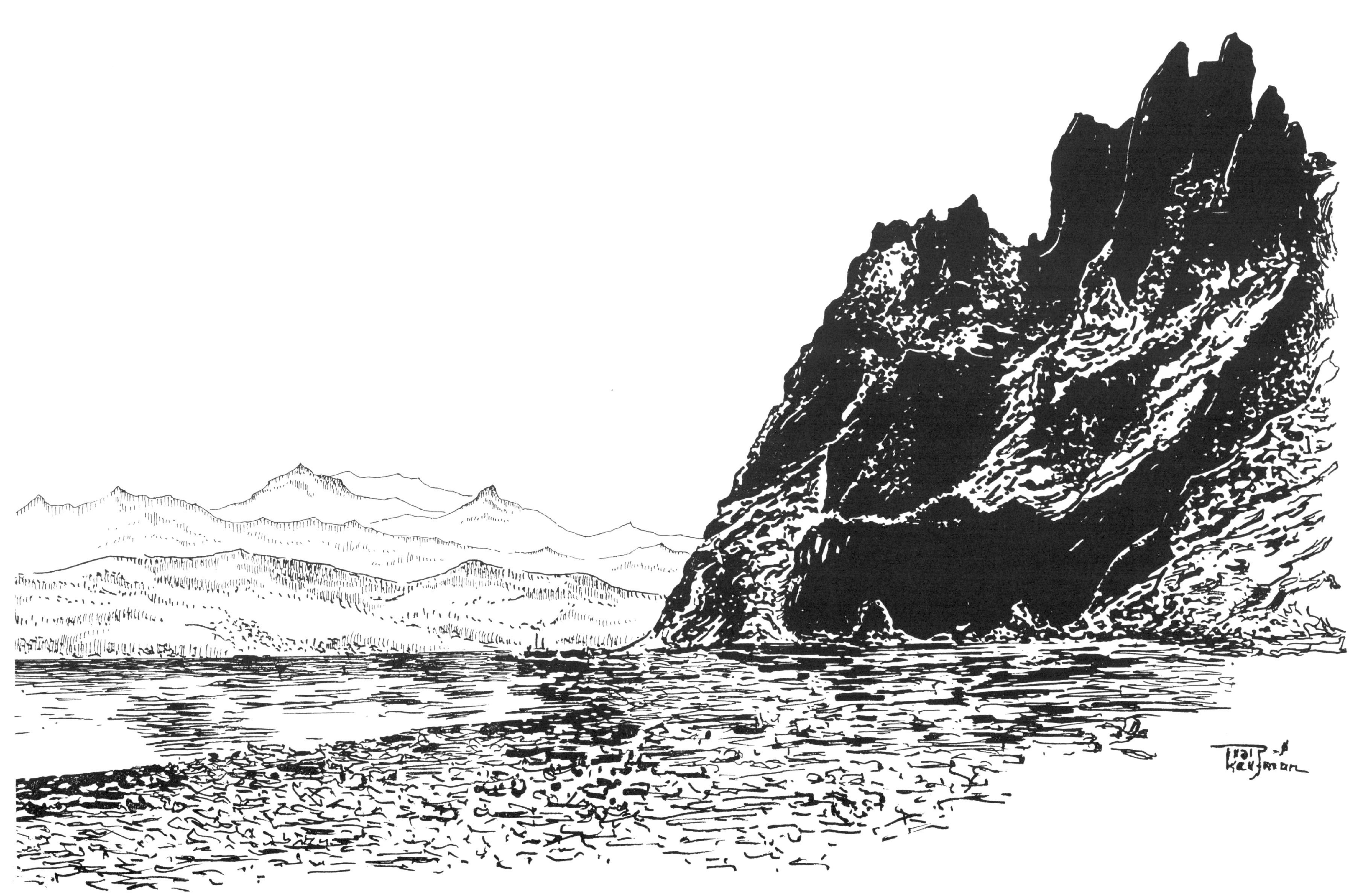

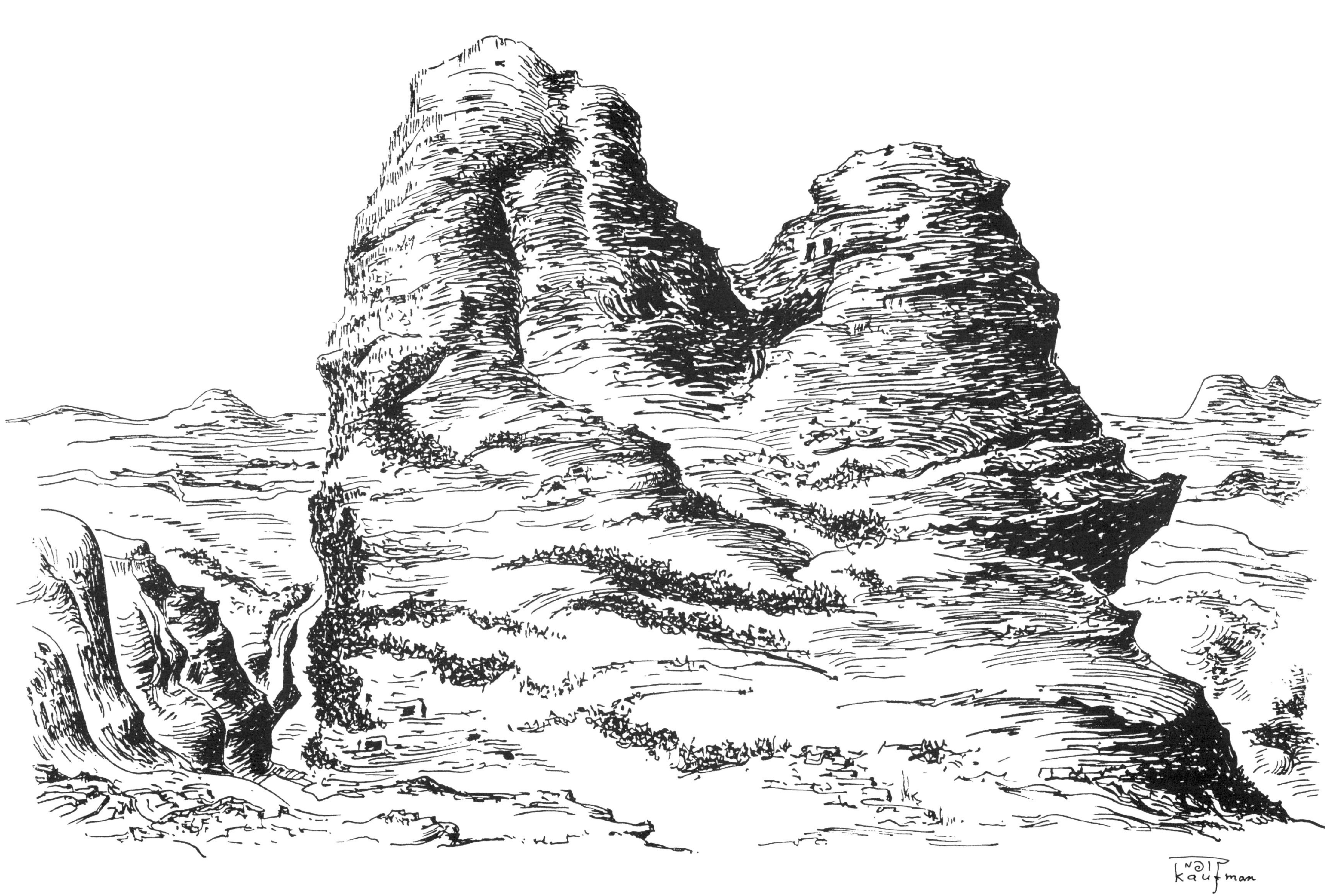
Kaufman

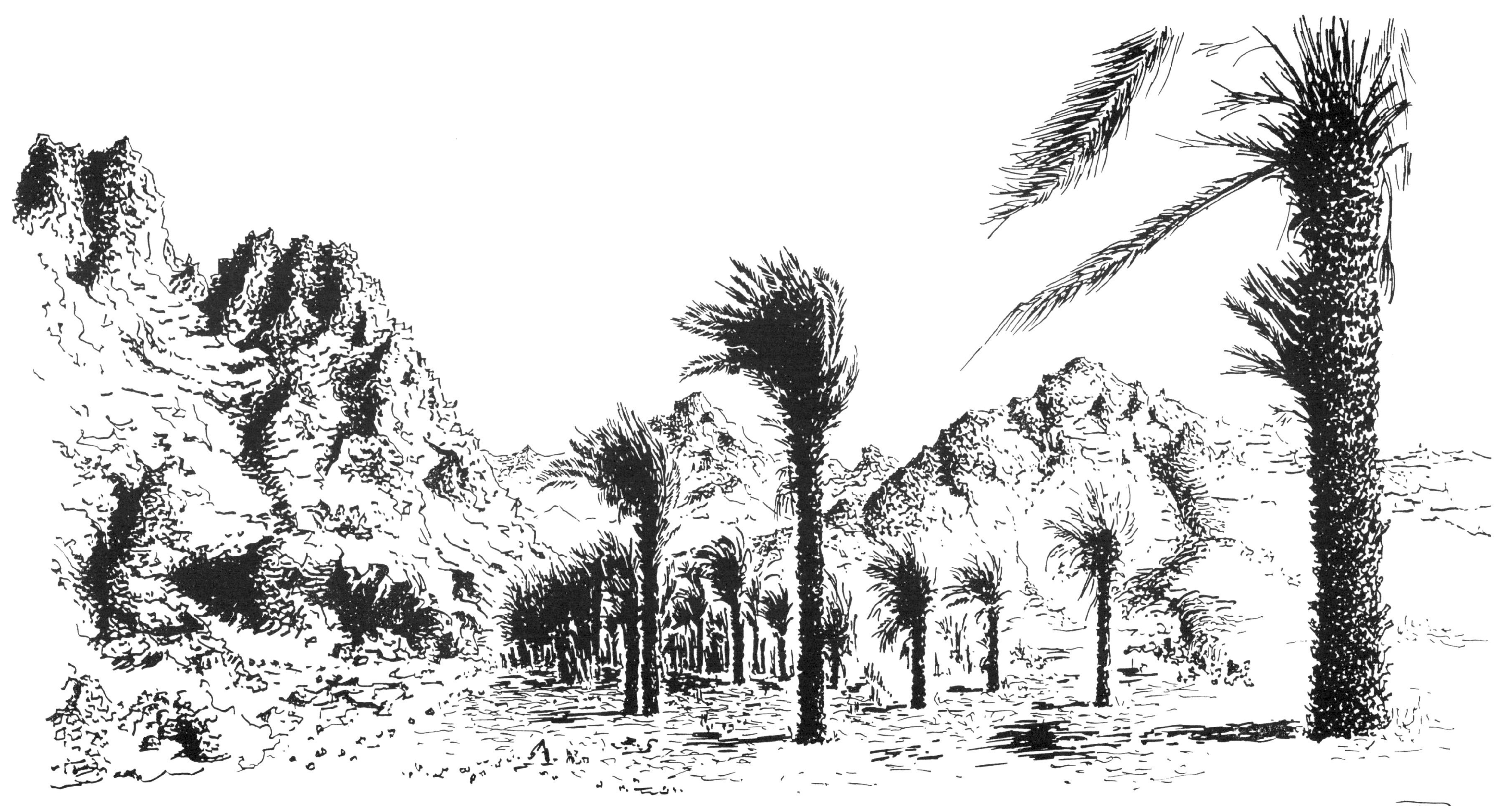
Kaufman

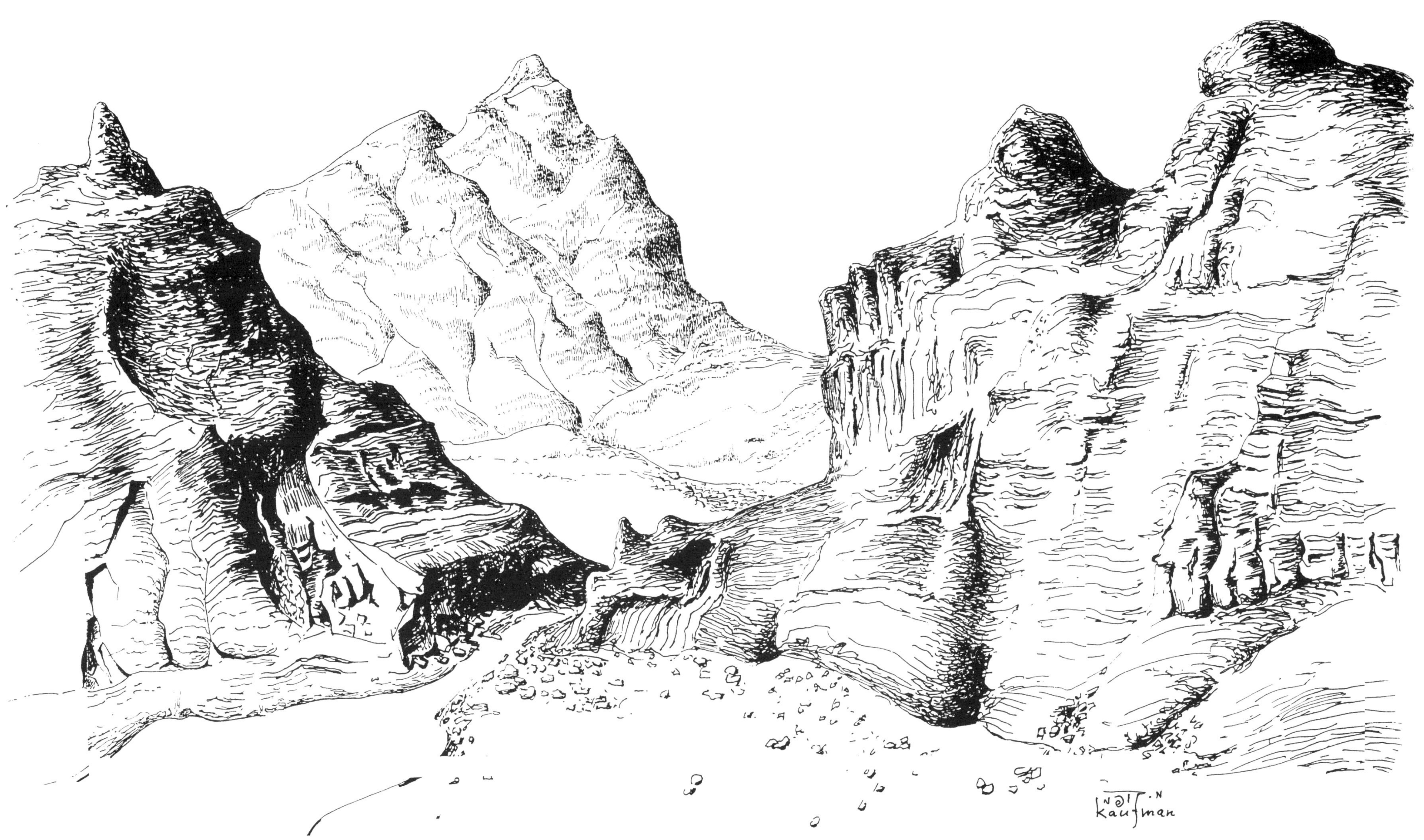
Kaufman